CW00864972

SIMPLE REFLECTIVE REFLECTIONS

Published Books

One Who Dared: Mary Lange … A Short Portrait (A Booklet)
Inspirational Musing
Adventures in Poetry
Words from the Heart
A Journey of Faith
Christmas is Every Day of the Year
A Woman Used By God
Poems about Mother Mary Lange, OSP

SIMPLE REFLECTIVE REFLECTIONS

Sr. Magdala Marie Gilbert, OSP

Library of Congress Control Number: 2019901602

ISBN:	Hardcover	978-1-7960-1535-5
	Softcover	978-1-7960-1536-2
	eBook	978-1-7960-1537-9

Print information available on the last page.

Rev. date: 02/22/2019

To order additional copies of this book, contact:
Xlibris
1-888-795-4274
www.Xlibris.com
Orders@Xlibris.com
790454

CONTENTS

CONTENTS

DEDICATED

To the sweet, sweet Holy Spirit under whose inspiration and guidance the author began to write down thoughts and insights, from her inner spirit.

PREFACE

These writings are a compilation of various thoughts and reflections that have been written throughout the years as well as some writings for the Catholic Review and "Keep On Teaching." "Keep On Teaching" is an enrichment program for Catechists in the Archdiocese of Baltimore and the surrounding Counties of Maryland including the Washington, DC and Philadelphia areas.

I once read somewhere that if you have something to say, write it down and publish it so that others may enjoy the experience too. It is said that it serves no purpose to have written things you think are worth-while, at least to you, sitting in some storage. So taking the advice of that wise person I decided to collect the worth-while pieces and put them in some sort of order. I think that some will be able to resonate with me in my musings about Jesus and life in general.

I am a simple soul, so no one needs to be afraid to read these pages and not be able to understand what is written here. Some might say that these writings are too simplistic but I will leave that up to the reader.

Giving all praise and honor to God for the inspiration of the blessed Holy Spirit for her guidance and inspiration; as I muse about my relationship with God and other people in my life.

May you the reader, be blessed as you read these pages. Any praise is to be given to the Lord. May God always be the beginning and end of all our praise.

WRITTEN WORDS

Written words take many roads
Some we need to see and trod
Others we need to circumvent
And find the ones that God sent.

Written words are like roads
They lead us to better goals
As we tread this road of life,
Keeping us free from bitter strife.

BIBLICAL THOUGHTS

CHAPTER 1

The Writings

The Pentateuch of the Bible consists of the Law (Torah), the Prophets (Major and Minor), and the Writings. The Writings (The Wisdom Books), in the Catholic Tradition added seven more books to the Bible, not in the Jewish tradition, nor in the Protestant Bible. The Psalms, Job, Proverbs, Song of Songs, 1 Chronicles, 2 Chronicles, and Lamentations were written in Hebrew. The added books are called, "Deuterocanonical" because they were not all written in Hebrew but mostly in Greek. These Books consists of Tobit (written in Armenian), Judith, and Wisdom of Solomon, Ecclesiastes, Beruch, 2 Maccabees and a few other writings. The meaning of deuterocanonical comes from the Greek meaning "belonging to the second canon." The word was first used in 1566 by a converted Jew, Sixtus of Siena.

For a long time these extra books were a point of argumentations among the early Fathers of the Church. Even St Jerome, who wrote the Vulgate Bible, although he used the Deutero, never publicly acknowledged that they were supposed to be an addition. He did not add them to his version of the Bible. Finally in 1546 at the Council of Trent, the controversy was settled. It was decreed that the Books were Sacred and Canonical and worthy to be added as a permanent fixture to the Bible.

The word canon is applied to Scripture and has a sacred and consecrated meaning. It is composed of the authoritative writing of the Church written under divine inspiration for the well being of the Church. The Deuterocanonical Book of the Bible is considered by the Church to be the canonical part of the Old Testament but not included in the Hebrew Bible.

The books were used for reflection, piety, and means of teaching us how to live good lives. They all seem to flow back to the Law (Torah) of giving honor and glory to God, how to treat our neighbors and our duty to God, (the Ten Commandments.)

The **Psalms** are considered one of the most used Writings of the Old Testament. The Psalms were considered for a long time to be the sole writing of King David. In later years it was known that other writers wrote psalms as well. It is thought that Moses, Solomon, the sons of Korah, the sons of Aesop to name a few wrote psalms as well. Some of the psalms have no known authors at all. Some seemed to have been written during the exile years of the Jews. No matter who wrote them, they are great sources of relief for anything that may trouble you. They bring peace, give comfort, are good for meditation, bring joy and console those who are grieving or for whatever else that might be bothering us in life.

There are 150 Psalms: the longest is Psalm 119 and the only one with 20 verses, the shortest is Psalm 117; Psalm 118 verse 8 is the middle of the Bible. Psalm 23 is one of the most used of the Bible. It seems to sooth the feelings of people in time of need. It is often used during funerals. It seems to have a calming effect on those who are in mourning. The Psalms are divided into Books.

The First Book --- Psalms 1 - 41
The Second Book --- Psalms 42 - 72
The Third Book --- Psalms 79 - 89
The Fourth Book --- Psalms 90 – 106
The Fifth Book --- Psalms 107 -150

Sometimes the Psalms overlap in content with other psalms: this however does not hinder their usefulness but rather ingrains the message into our heads and hearts. The Psalms are used each day in the Liturgy of the Word as the Responsorial Psalm and in Para-Liturgical Services on various occasions. The Psalms are also used in books that are used by religious men and women called the Liturgy of the Hours. These prayers are recited Morning, Noon, Evening and at Night.

The **Book of Job is** a poem that is meant to teach a moral lesson, set in prose. It is sometimes called the most difficult book in the Bible. This book attempts to pit good against evil with good triumphing.

Job was a man of great wealth, one day the Devil challenged God to let him have his way with Job to test and see if Job really was as good and trusting in God as he seemed. God agreed to this. Subsequently Job lost all that he owned, wealth as well as all his children. Job's friends came to try to console him but end up telling him to curse God and die. Job trusted in the Lord and was rewarded in time by gaining back all lost wealth. Job remained faithful and was rewarded for his faithfulness. What God did for Job, God can and will do for us if we are in the same predicament. God knows no partiality; we are all precious in his sight.

Job is a lesson for us all to follow, that when things get tough continue to trust in God no matter what. He is seen as a type of Christ or the Suffering Messiah. This book also teaches us that when misfortune comes it is not a sign of God's wrath.

Proverbs are considered by many to be written solely by Solomon, the son of David, King of Israel. Solomon was known for his wisdom, so many of the Proverbs are attributed to him. However, other minor writers also wrote but because Solomon was a King, they gave the credit to him. For many years this book was know as "The Book of Wisdom." It is easy to think so, because it acts like a "wisdom" book. The Book of Proverbs is divided thus:

1. Introduction: The Value of Wisdom
2. First Collection of the Proverbs of Solomon
3. Sayings of the Wise
4. Other Sayings of the Wise
5. Second Collections of the Proverbs of Solomon
6. The Words of Agar
7. Numerical Proverbs
8. The Words of Lemuel

The primary aim of Proverbs is one of teaching and learning. We might call this a teaching book. Proverbs are wise sayings and admonitions relating to the morality of all of God's people. Much of it is relegated to the admonition of the young and those inexperienced with life. This book wants to direct the listeners to live clean, moral and fruitful lives. The book takes in a wide spectrum of subjects. Each country has its own set of Proverbs.

Ecclesiastes, in Hebrew it is called Qoheleth, meaning one who calls forth an assembly to proclaim some truth. It is concerned with the value of human life and that all things are vain. No matter how much money you have, or prestige, nothing matters except the union you have with God and your ability to stay connected to God. This can be attained by staying in the will of God and not putting our trust in things, for all things are temporary and passing. Qoheleth does all the talking in this book.

King Solomon has been given the title as author of this work but it has been found that much of the writings were done after his time. It really does not matter who really wrote this book, suffice it to say that it is a great addition to the Bible and God is to be praised for allowing the Church to continue to look at this book of the Bible and use it from time to time. The Book of Ecclesiastes consists of three parts:

Part I - Vanity in ones private life
Part II - Vanity in civil life
Part III – Vanity in thinking you are full of Wisdom

Song of Songs, quiet poetic in nature, was one of three Books attributed to King Solomon. It is one of the shortest books in the Bible. This book describes the mutual love of a man and a woman. It is their song of love to each other. The song was sung as they were preparing for the marriage bed. Various meanings have been attributed to the Song of Songs. Some say it is strictly sexual while the Church equates it to the love of Christ for the Church. It is considered a marriage between God and the people of God.

The Song of Songs is not mentioned by name in the New Testament as such, but is alluded to in some passages in the New Testament e.g. Matt. 9:15 – John 3:29. Art and Music have been composed using the Song of Songs. The Black Madonna is a case in point using the passage, "Thou art Black and beautiful O daughter of Jerusalem (Songl:5). Some modern songs have been written using materials from the Song of Songs. Pope Benedict XVI in his Encyclical "Deus Caritas Est" (God is Love) in 2006, referred to the Song of Songs as both literal and allegorical. He states that erotic love (***eros***) and self-donating love (***agape***) are shown as the two halves of true love, both giving and receiving.

Reflections from an Africentric Perspective

As African Americans, it seemed as a people, the Books of Writing were always with us even before we became aware of that section of the Bible. We always knew that you must honor your mother or something bad would happen to you. There was a saying in our house that if you did not go to Church you would lose your blessings and that the elderly were full of wisdom and we should respect and honor them. It was instilled into us that you did not put your business in the "streets," it showed a lack of disrespect for your family, if you did. Our African ancestors made good use of proverbs in their daily lives, they sounded quite a lot like Proverbs and other tenets of the Wisdom Books. The tales of the slave Aesop, who had great wit and wisdom, lived around 620 BC, have always been a part of our lives. His wisdom dealt with the human condition seen through the eyes of animals.

The most used section of **THE WRITINGS** are the Psalms, especially Psalm 23, "The Lord is My Shepherd" which is used when troubles come and we go to God for comfort in union with Psalm 27, "The Lord is My Light" also a comforting psalm. Psalm 23 is used very often in our liturgy at funerals. The Book of Job has been useful in the African American Community. When the Lord seems to send so much trouble and discord into our lives we remember the story of Job and how he trusted God in spite of all his adversity. The main focus in this is that African Americans know that what God did for the Hebrews He will do for us. We trust God to fulfill His promises and as we read the works of Solomon and other authors of the **WRITINGS** we connect because their story is our story.

We can readily apply these sayings from the sages to our own particular situation because we know, like the Hebrews, what it is like to be an alien in a foreign land. Thus we apply these "Wisdom" sayings to our own daily experiences.

References Used:

1. The Holy Bible – Published for the Josephites: Todays English Version with deuterocanonical/Apocrypha by – American Bible Society @ 1999. Used with permission.
2. The Catholic Encyclopedia - Volume III, Robert Appleton Company, by George J. Reid; published in New York, 1905.

CHAPTER 2

The Story of Esther

The story of Esther takes place in Babylon. Years before Esther was born Nebuchadnezzar, King of Babylon, captured the Jewish people from Jerusalem and brought them to Babylon. There the Jewish people became the servants of the Babylonians. Esther, a young Jewish girl, lived in Babylon with her cousin, Mordecai, who adopted her after her parents died, as his daughter. They lived in the city of Susa. He was in good standing with the Persian King Ahasuerus also known as King Xerxes and served at his court. One night Mordecai had a dream about someone killing the King. He reported this to the king who apprehended the persons. This gave Esther's cousin a firm standing in the palace and with the King.

There was a man at the palace named Haman who hated the Jewish people and plotted to have all of them killed. This man's hatred of the Jewish people knew no bounds. His hatred of the Jews was much like some white people's attitude toward black people.

One day the King gave a great feast for seven days for all the people, poor and rich alike in the surrounding city of Susa. During the feasting the King asked his queen, Queen Vashti to join him. She refused and was deposed as queen because of her arrogance.

King Xerxes had to find another queen so they brought to him many young ladies to choose from and after the trial period, Esther won his heart and he chose Esther to be his queen. Prompted by Mordecai, Esther did reveal to the king that she was Jewish.

As time passed Haman's plot to kill the Jewish people started to unfold. Mordecai sat in sack cloth and ashes to pray for deliverance and sent word to Esther to talk to the king, reminding her that if she did not, she too would be killed. So Esther took off her fine clothes along with her household and fasted and prayed.

After her period of fasting Esther put on her fine garments and went into the courtyard of the King. Seeing her looking worried he asked what the matter was. Here was her chance to tell the King about the plot of Haman.

Queen Easter gave a banquet one night and Haman was invited. At the banquet Esther laid out the plot of Haman to kill her people. The King was amazed at this revelation and ordered Haman to be hung on the very gibbet that he had planned for Mordecai, whom he detested because he would not rise when he walked by to pay him homage.

Haman's house was given to Easter and she revealed to the king her relationship to Mordecai. The King gave Mordecai, Haman's ring and charge of his household. Later, alone with the King, Esther asked the king to renounce the edict that Haman had enacted against her people. The King complied. They then became masters of their enemies.

Esther was not afraid.

Esther put her life in jeopardy for the sake of her Jewish people. Even though she was afraid of the King, she risked all to have an audience with him. She could have been killed for being so bold. Sometimes, however we have to be bold when it is the right thing to do.

During slavery, people like Harriet Tubman risked their lives to save hundreds of Black people. Esther reminds us of Harriet Tubman, Rosa Parks and Martin Luther King, Jr. for their boldness for freedom and love for their people.

This story affirms Black people when we were in trouble especially when we would try to protect each other like Mordecai, when he sent word to Queen Esther to reveal the plot of Haman against the Jewish people to King Xerxes. When she hesitated because she was queen and did not want to get involved, Mordecai reminded her that if the Jewish people perished she would perish also. Living in a beautiful palace with pretty clothes and many servants would not save her. Truth is its own reward.

What Mordecai was telling her is that they must stick together, to be divided meant total disaster. For us too, as Black people, what happens to one black person should concern us all. What is done to one black person should be the concern of all of us. If one person is denigrated, we all are denigrated. This truth does not only refer to Black people only but to other people who are persecuted because of race, belief or gender.

A Graced Moment

A graced moment of conversion is that moment in time when one sees a situation that seems hopeless and turns it over to God and believes that God who can do all things, will make things right. One then gives one's life and situation to God who will work it all out for us. God loves us very much and when we turn our life over to him he will reward our faith.

Is Racism an Issue in these United States?

Although many in these United States think that racism is not an issue any more, think again. Keep up with the daily or nightly news and you will see. We still need to teach our youth the value of education, the value of family and race so that they will not be deluded into thinking that all is well. We have to be as astute as Mordecai was with Esther. We must preach the whole truth and keep our eyes and ears open to the insidious snare of the evil of racism in our modern world. This world would tell us that traditions and concern for the race is old fashioned. Telling our story over and over is of great value in the process of tradition and evangelization. In all of this we must come to the conclusion that no matter how we are treated we are all children of the same God.

Tell the Story

Tell the story over and over
Tell it till we all get to glory
Be not afraid of world opinion
We won't be anyone's minion.

Tell the story over and over
Preach till it reaches the cliffs of Dover
God is our true anchor while here
So tell your story without fear.

Tell the story over and over.
Tell it 'till we all get to glory.

If we do not tell the story and tell the true truth, then future generations will be lost because we have not passed the story on to them. Let us take a lesson from Mordecai and teach our children what it means to be family as he taught Esther. We must tell the story of slavery and how we as a people got over. That God loves us as he loves all His children no matter their race.

What in the story can promote the Sacred and connect with the secular?

When Mordecai and Esther found themselves in trouble they begged the Lord to help them and show them the way. However, they knew they had duties to fulfill and so Esther tended to her household and Queenly duties while Mordecai fulfilled the task of being the right hand of King Xerxes. They were able to be both a true servant of God and a true servant of their adopted country.

We too have the same opportunity to serve God and country by being good citizens and stewards. As Christians we demonstrate this each day by serving God through service to our neighbor and giving God his special day on Sundays and special Holy Days. God will reward our love and give us the grace to persevere.

CHAPTER 3

The Widow Of Zarephath

1 Kings 17: 8-24

Elijah was a prophet of God in Israel. He was sent to a town named Zarephath. God was teaching Elijah little by little what he, God, wanted Elijah to do. He was learning slowly what God wanted him to do. God had promised a drought throughout the land. It was Elijah's duty to prepare the people for the disaster. A drought is a period of time when there is no rain, the water supply is depleted. People are in dire need of water. God sends hard times to the earth from time to time to remind the people that they should focus on God and not on people or things. If there is no water there are no crops. Food and water are scarce and hard to get.

Elijah attached himself to a woman of Zarephath who was focusing on fixing something for herself and her son and preparing for death. She saw no other recourse because of the drought. He asked her to fix a little cake for him to eat and get him a little water to drink, and then prepared food for herself and her son. He promised her that everything would be alright. The woman believed and fed Elijah. Because of her belief, God took care of them until the drought ended. The Lord also rewarded the faith of the woman by letting Elijah save her son who had fallen ill unto death. Elijah, through the grace of God, brought the son back to life.

Just as Elijah heeded the voice of God so must we. God has a plan for each of us. Even though at the time, we do not know what the plan is, in God's good time, the plan for us will be revealed. Elijah went where he was sent on faith. All we have to do when the revelation is revealed is be still and listen to God's voice. God sends miracles in our lives daily. We too can be other Elijah's by being attentive to those around us. We can be used just as effectively as Elijah. It may not be performing a big miracle but we can perform small miracles by donating needed items to charities, helping with scholarships, providing school supplies to poor children or giving money to reputable charities. We can become aware of the need of those around us, loving one another by being present to them and offering our help when needed. In this way, ***when God speaks to you, you must receive it, even if you are not sure. God will reveal it to you and if you trust and believe... You can be the "center of a miracle to come."***

Transforming/Defining moments of Faith of Elijah

This story can be very liberating if we believe that God can do anything. We can imitate Elijah by obeying the will of God for us. Elijah did not always know what God wanted him to do, but he put his faith in God and knew from experience that God would take care of business. Like Elijah and the Widow all we have to do is allow God to use us, by following the rules and advice God gives us through the Commandments, the Beatitudes and the laws of the Church. We know that we are not alone in this universe and have ample opportunities to be the Hand of God to our neighbor. As Black people, we know that God has our back. God has brought us from slavery and through all kinds of evils. As God has helped us to overcome much evil so we too have to continue to fight for justice, especially for those who cannot help themselves. We must not be afraid to name evil when we see it and try to rectify that evil no matter where it is found. God wants us to take care of each other as God cares for us. ***"You have to hold on even if you cannot see what the end will be."***

God will send us seemingly difficult tasks and we may not want to do them, but as Christians we must follow God's lead. Thus when we see the face of racism we are to name it. We do not turn our heads and say that it does not concern us. Whatever we see that which is not of God and know that the issue should be addressed then we are to address it. We are to address sin, even when we cannot see what the end will be. Sometimes we have to wait on the Lord to tell us what to do, like Elijah. Then we follow our conscience and act as God's children.

God expects us to be other evangelizers. Elijah was an evangelizer, although he did not see himself as such. We are our sister's and brother's keepers. We are to bring others to a belief in God and show them by word and action how great our God is. Our mission in life as Christians is to be announcers to others about this good God of ours. Sometimes we can evangelize by leading good Christian lives, by inviting others to follow Christ and by being ministers of Catechesis. Like Elijah, with the help of God, we can even bring the spiritually dead back to life. Working with others on our jobs is a good time to converse with others about our faith or just about something we read in the Bible. We can share our faith with others socially as well. We can form a prayer group with others, be it family, fellow workers or friends. Often when people see Jesus in us, then their lives will change. We can talk up Jesus any place, any time. Did not our ancestors have Church in the cotton fields or at night would steal off and go by the river and have Church? Many were converted in those still night hours as they sang, "Take me to the water, take me to the water, take me to the water, to be baptized." Our ancestors held on even when they could not see what the end would be. Can we do less?

CHAPTER 4

Faithfulness In Persistent Prayer

Matthew 15:21-28...*Then Jesus went from that place and withdrew to the region of Tyre and Sidon. And behold a Canaanite woman of that District came and cried out, "Have pity on me, Lord, Son of David! My daughter is tormented by a demon." But Jesus did not say a word to answer her. The disciples came and begged him, "Send her away, for she keeps calling out after us." Jesus said in reply, "I was sent to the lost sheep of the house of Israel." But the woman came and did Jesus homage, saying Lord, "Help me," Jesus said, "It is not right to take the food of the children and throw it to the dogs. She said, "Please, Lord, for even the dogs eat the scraps that fall from the table of their masters." Then Jesus said to her in reply, "O woman great is your faith! Let it be done to you as you wish." And her daughter was healed from that hour.*

Jesus preached in many places then finally ended up in the region of Tyre and Sidon which was very providential. Jesus goes where the need is greatest. He came to earth for one reason, to bring Salvation to the lost, not only to the lost sheep of Israel, but to all the peoples of the world.

Jesus chose disciples to teach them the way to the Kingdom as well as how to be compassionate after He was gone from them. The Apostles did not often understand what Jesus was trying to teach them. But being the good God that He was, Jesus put up with their whining, bickering, impatience and ignorance.

The region that Jesus and the apostles found themselves in was not a Jewish town. So when they found a woman crying out after them, they should not have been surprised. Did the same thing not happen to them in the towns of Bethany, Jerusalem, Cana, Galilee and other Jewish regions?

The Canaanite woman was very brave in her insistence for healing on behalf of her daughter. Nothing Jesus said would deter her from her mission, to have her daughter healed, even being liken to a dog. Jesus had a mother and knew how His own mother was going to feel at His crucifixion. So Jesus felt her pain and had pity by healing the woman's daughter. **Jesus came into the world to set us free, to liberate us from sin, darkness and confusion**...

The Canaanite woman wanted only one thing from Jesus, to deliver her daughter from the demon that possessed her. What about our demons? Do we try as this woman to rid ourselves of our demon? What are the demons in our lives and the lives of the people whom we encounter? What means are we using to help get the demons out of our lives? Have we tried Jesus? All of this requires deep faith.

Being of another nationality or race did not prevent Jesus from showing pity for this woman. Although it seemed that he was only catering to the Jewish nation, yet Jesus knew that all peoples are children of God. They say that the Canaanite people were people of color, the off-spring of Noah's son Ham. The healing of the woman's daughter shows that God shows no partiality. All we have to do is ask for what we need. If we do not get the answer we seek, ask again, again and again. God does not look at color, if so that woman's daughter would not have been healed. What Jesus did for her He will do for each of us. Jesus died for all races.

Although the Canaanite woman was not Jewish, but a woman of color, she felt that Jesus was the Messiah and that He could do for her what he had done for so many people. She knew he could cure her daughter. She believed! We must believe and follow the way of Jesus. Although, at times we do not feel worthy, yet we must persist. Faith shows us that God loves all of His children.

Anyone who hears this story knows that this woman was not going to keep quiet about Jesus healing her daughter. That is what we must do when the story is too good to keep to ourselves. Our goal as Christians is to spread the Good News. We, as a people, are good at spreading news of our faith in Jesus: so we must continue to speak out like this Canaanite sister.

In Scripture we learn about this faith-filled Canaanite woman and her persistent pleading. Unafraid of ridicule she yelled out her request. Sunday after Sunday we hear the Good News of Jesus, come Monday morning we forget about the teaching from Sunday. We forget that Sunday and the days of the week are together. Religion and our everyday existence go hand in hand, it is a **both/and** situation. We have to practice what we heard on Sunday from the pulpit on Monday, Tuesday and throughout the week.

Usually the races did not mix in the time of Jesus. The Canaanite woman was in her own territory when Jesus and the Apostles intruded on her turf. Although she felt a bit intimidated by Jesus and the Twelve Apostles she took her chances and became bold to ask a favor of Jesus. Although she knew the Apostles did not like her calling out after then yet she persisted until Jesus granted her request. She was not intimidated or afraid. As people of color (or if you are not a person of color) we too must insist on justice we must have faith in Jesus. We have to be unafraid and not allow ourselves to be intimidated either by the civil authorities or the Church.

First of all the town where Jesus and the Apostles stopped were towns of the decedents of Ham. It showed that Jesus sought out that particular town because Jesus knew that there was a need for His presence. The faith of this woman drew Jesus to that place. Jesus was not impressed by nationality, creed or race. Someone needed Him and He responded.

The moment of conversion comes when we can say yes to a situation. Conversion is a radical change from one state of being to another. It is a time when we have such faith in God that nothing can dissuade us from our opinion. No amount of shushing from the Apostles could hush that Canaanite sister. We too must be changed from our own self-centeredness and follow the lead of Jesus. We should not only carry the good News but **"WE"** must be the Good News.

Never give up on God no matter what. If we have faith we will be victorious. God will never forsake or abandon us even when we think God is saying no. This Canaanite woman is a good example of never giving up. So strong was her faith that her prayer was heard. We must have that same strong faith, even though Jesus referred to her as a dog, she did not give up.

Keep close to Jesus; call on Him in time of need.

Call upon Jesus when times are rough. People will not understand but that is alright. If we keep our eyes on Jesus everything will work out. Sometimes we get into a rut and need help, ask Jesus or a good friend to help, everything will come together. God sends us friends to assist us in our time of need, use them. We must learn to lean on one another under the guidance of the Holy Spirit. Jesus wants us to ask for help. God put people on earth and in our lives to help one another. We must remember, though, that God is always in charge.

CHAPTER 5

Conversion of the Ethiopian Eunuch

Acts 8: 26-38

Philip, minding his own business was approached by an Angel to go down a certain route to Gaza. I am sure he was amazed but obeyed and set out for Gaza. There he found an Ethiopian Eunuch, an official of the Candace in his carriage. Candace was a royal title in Ethiopia, relegated to the Queen. Because of a long connection of the Ethiopians with the Jewish people the Eunuch had just come back from worshiping in Jerusalem.

It is said that long ago King Solomon had an affair with the Queen of Ethiopia and bore a son who went one day to Palestine and stole the Ark of the Covenant. The tale is... that they still have it to this day. This Jewish connection is current to this very day.

As the Eunuch was reading scripture, he came across a passage he did not understand. The passage was from the book of Isaiah, which read, "*Like a sheep led to slaughter, and as a lamb before its shearer is silent, so, opened not his mouth. In his humiliation justice was denied him. Who will tell of his posterity? For his life is taken from the earth.*" (Isaiah 53; 7-8-10). This passage was paraphrased for the sake of brevity. One can find the entire text in (Isaiah. 53.).

When Philip came up to his carriage he asked Philip of whom was the writer speaking, of himself or someone else? Here Philip opened up the scripture passage for him so that he understood that the writer was speaking not of himself but about Jesus. Seeing water near-by, the Eunuch asked if he could be baptized and it was done.

Personal Conversion

The Eunuch was in earnest. He asked Philip what the words he was reading really meant. The Holy Spirit inspired Philip with the right words to say. The Eunuch, in hearing the words of Philip, was set free. Now he knew what the words meant. In understanding the message he asked to be baptized.

We know that the words of the Gospel should be liberating and so they liberated the Eunuch from his ignorance and set him free. As baptized Christians we too were freed by our baptism to be able to absorb the word of God and spread it abroad. The Good News is not to be kept to ourselves but shared.

The Eunuch did not keep his conversion to himself. He could not wait to get to Ethiopia to share his message with his people, to tell all about the good news of Jesus. Are we like this Eunuch, anxious to spread the good news to family, friends, co-workers and acquaintances? When we hear the truth about Jesus, are our lives changed by hearing the message?

Philip's words moved the Eunuch to listen with rapt attention. Do we do the same on Sunday? Or do we listen to the Word and are so moved? Or are we hurrying to get to the ball game, watch TV, and go to the Mall or the like?

We must never get tired of the Gospel and its implication for our lives and that of others. We take the place of Jesus walking among his people. We will be the only message about Jesus that some people will ever get to know. The Ethiopian Eunuch not only told his family the good news but every one he met. In fact it is said that he converted a whole nation. How about that for Evangelization? He used only his voice. In these ultra modern times we have many more avenues with which to spread the Good News.

Use Me Lord

If God can use such a man how much more can He use us, who have all this modern technology to get the work out in one swoop, using television and the internet! Some of us are good writers, so how about the written word and other resources like DVD's, CD's, newspapers, use of libraries, computers with email and forwards. We, in this modern generation have money and technology to get the message out. We have no excuse to not evangelize.

God does not expect the impossible from us, all he wants from us is to use the means we have at our disposal to make him known and loved. And in the doing, try to make this world a better place because we lived in it.

I am sure when the Eunuch went to worship each day or whenever they worshiped at that time and era, that he and others did not look bored. I can envision the Eunuch telling and retelling his story to anyone and everyone who would listen. That must be us. We must tell and retell the story of Jesus, never tiring and living our lives so that people see only Jesus in us.

Being a good Christian does not mean that we cannot have a good time, go to the movies, games and other fun things. We can do all that and still have Jesus in our hearts and be examples to our peers.

The Ethiopian Eunuch

Ebon of skin so handsome and strong
The Ethiopian Eunuch rode meditatively along.
Hovering over scripture passages
In his chariot, reading... musing... alone
Of Isaiah who wrote sacred messages.
Pillar of the Candace
Influential and true to his race
Accounting to the most high God
Noting God's love of us all, and who
sometimes spare the rod.

Evaluating his life of service
Untiring and giving servant
Never thinking of the self
Undying love of his ministry
Counting on God who is infinity
Honoring all by his call to proclaim, the
Word made Flesh for all eternity.

Our Heritage

As people of Color we know what it is to rely on the Lord for all our needs. We have always been spontaneous and ready to share our faith with other people. Some of us may have forgotten how we used to say "I'm going to Mass on Sunday. Want to come?" We need to get back into the habit of inviting. There is a difference between inviting and harassing. We evangelize, like the Eunuch, by both words and examples. Let us not be ashamed of being Black and Catholic. Our ancestors were in the Bible long before other races that inhabit the earth today. Like the Eunuch, as baptized Christians, let us own this faith of ours and share it with others. We must be evangelizers.

CHAPTER 6

Saint Paul …
Apostle to the Gentiles

Struck by lightning to save his soul…

While listening to a Christian Radio Program, one day, one of the commentators said, "You know that Paul, before his conversion, was an evil man." That really threw me. But when you really think about it he was not really an evil person. He was misguided by some of the erroneous teaching of the Jewish hierarchy or priestly class of the Jews. Through their instigation Paul went around rounding up Christians, having them thrown into prison, consenting to have Christians killed by any means possible. In those days many were stoned to death like St. Stephen. Before they would stone someone they would lay their cloaks at the feet of the instigator; this time it was Saul. Saul, as he was called in those days. I suppose to keep their clothing from getting blood on them, not knowing that the blood of the Christians was still on their hands and souls. Yes, Saul was really, really a very misguided man who did evil acts in his zeal for the Jewish tradition.

But then the hand of Jesus touched Saul whose name was changed from Saul to Paul after being knocked from his horse and putting some horse sense into his misguided head. Meeting Jesus on that road to Damascus was life changing for Paul. Paul was given orders to go and bring those erroneous people called Christians back to stand trial for their beliefs. As Paul was on his way to catch and kill Christians, he was knocked from his horse. Jesus appeared to him. A holy man in the city of Damascus was guided by the Holy Spirit to go to the place where Paul was staying and restore sight to Paul. When the light struck him on the road it blinded him. God really got his attention.

I suppose many of us can relate to the man Saul. We want to have our own way instead of allowing Jesus to lead and guide us. We think we have it all together… nobody can tell me what to do . . . I am my own person. Just leave me alone to do my own thing.

But if we are like the converted Paul, we will allow Jesus to use us like a fork or spoon. We are no longer our own but Jesus is the beginning and the end for us. We will be more tolerant, charitable, loving and forgiving. However, if we have erred like Paul we can always come back to Jesus and say we are sorry and continue from there to be that person God created us to be.

We would be like St. Paul leaving all things behind adhering to Jesus and Jesus alone. Nothing will be too hard. We can say like the song, "And he will bear you up on eagles' wings." If Jesus has you in His corner what or who is there to fear? Life will become bearable, things will not get you down and what people say to you or about you is as dirt to be swept up with a brush and pan and thrown into the trash can. You will be able to say with St. Paul, *"Who then can separate us from the love of Christ?"*

(Romans 8: 35). "I say, "Nothing."

Saint Paul went on to be counted among the Apostle. Although Paul did not walk with Jesus in the beginning, he learned through prayer and study. The lesson for us here is that it does not depend on the length of time we have served the Church but our zeal. That no matter when we embrace Christ and His teaching that time is not a factor. All Christ wants of us is faithfulness and a tenacity to do all we can to bring others to Gospel values. Zeal for Christ after his conversion ate Paul up. He could not do enough for Christ and his mission. He got into some heated arguments with some of the Apostles because of his zeal for Christ. They soon learned that this man was on fire for the Lord. By Paul's attitude, they were urged to step back and give him room to complete the task Jesus had given him to accomplish

We can learn a great lesson from Paul. When you are given a task to do, do it with gusto and try to bring others on board with you. After Paul's conversion, nothing was too difficult for him to do. Neither shipwreck, storm nor a snake bite could deter Paul from his mission.

One feature I liked about Paul was that he kept up with the people he had helped to convert, He would write letters urging them to remain steadfast in their faith. Today we have it so much easier. There are various mediums we can use to encourage someone we have helped along the way.

LETTERS TO THE HEBREWS

There is speculation among some scholars that this letter to the Hebrews is not really the work of Saint Paul but of someone else. Catholic scholars seem to believe this, so it is now a book on its own merit.

The Letter to the Hebrews in this version of the Bible is divided into ten main divisions, namely:

A. Introduction: Christ the complete revelation of God 1.1-3
B. Christ's superiority over the Angels 1.4-2.18
C. Christ's superiority over Moses and Joshua 3.1-4.13
D. The Superiorly of Christ's priesthood 4.14-7.28
E. The Superiorly of Christ's covenant 8.1-9.22
F. The Superiorly of Christ's sacrifice 9.23-10.39
G. The primacy of faith 11.1. - 12.29
H. Pleasing God 13.19
I. Closing prayer 13.20-21
J. Final Words 13.22-25

The Letter to the Hebrews constantly exhorted the Jewish Christians to live disciplined lives through frequent references to faithful people like Moses, from passages in the Old Testament. Many examples of obedience are cited throughout the chapters to spur the Jewish Christians on to become faith-filled disciples. They were spurred on to holiness of life, to overcome temptations and to discipline themselves through intentional sacrifices.

The emphasis placed on Jesus as Savior and High Priest was used to entice the Christians to greater love of Jesus and neighbor. That Jesus was greater than all the prophets and even the angels. The letter to the Hebrews was to place such emphasis on the love of Jesus for them; and his faithfulness, through his birth, death and resurrection, that they would want to do all they could to emulate his life and example.

During the time of the Hebrew people there were many nations larger than theirs. God felt pity for them and decided to take them under His protection. No matter what the Hebrews did, God was there to bail them out. We are a small minority like the Hebrews. The Lord adopted us because he heard our cry in slavery just as he heard the Hebrew people's cry in their captivity in Egypt. Although we are not in captivity and slavery now, we still need the help of God. We can rely on God's mercy to liberate us from sin by his love and mercy. In Hebrews it was attested that God loved us above the angels and that he sent Jesus to ransom us from sin and death.

God loves all of his children but has a special place in his heart for the down trodden and poor in this world. God has given us all the goods of creation for our use and as Black people we have to claim this legacy and honor the earth. We have to know that what God did for the Hebrews he will do for us. All we have to do is claim what is ours. God loves us as we are and we must never forget this love.

Because God loves us so much he wants us to live up to our potentials as Christians. As the Letter to the Hebrews admonished the Christians about living in peace, having compassion and love towards all, so must we. Just because the Predominant Race seems to have the upper hand does not mean that we have to hate them. We have to show everyone love as Jesus taught us. If we keep the commandments and precepts of God we will be rewarded in the end for loving others as Jesus loved us. It is not easy but with the grace and mercy of Jesus we can overcome.

The Letter to the Hebrews encouraged the followers of Jesus to take heart and not give scandal to their neighbors. This also applies to us. We have the mandate to bring others to follow Jesus by our good examples and courage in the midst of controversy and opposition. We must copy

Christ who was the first true evangelizer. We are all called to conversion of heart, to love no matter our race or origin. It is a mandate from God.

As we venture into the workplace we have to be ever mindful of our duty as Christians to give authentic witness. It does not mean that we have to get on a soapbox and shout the gospel but we must live the gospel, without using words. We do it with our actions. We have to be good employees or employers, in whatever our calling in life and meld job and faith into one. Our ancestors knew how to blend the secular and sacred together because of their bondage. We can do the same in our business transactions as we work and pray.

ALL

PATHS

LEAD

TO

JESUS

CHAPTER 7

Signs of Hope

Hope is a word that means having confidence in someone or something. In signs of hope there is a belief or faith that things will move and get better. We can find hope even within the shadows and sorrows of our lives. Signs of hope are always present in the Word of God. Even when God is angry with us we can count on His grace and mercy. When Adam and Eve sinned in the Garden of Eden God was angry that they had disobeyed him but he relented of total abandonment and promised to send a Savior to redeem the world after the fall. Jesus is our hope in the midst of chaos and confusion. With God there is always hope. He sends us signs of hope every day, all we have to do is be alert to our many blessings.

Saint Paul in (2 Cor.3:12) says that, "*Hope helps us to act boldly.*" It is something which we can look forward to. But this hope implies that we believe in a Divine being. We hope for many things. We hope that our neighborhood, our economy and the world will get better. What are we doing to make it so? We hope to have money to do things that will make us happy. We hope for a better tomorrow. We hope that our favorite person will become president or that we will become rich someday, that someday you will become famous in sports. If you are young ladies, you might hope to become models, singers, actresses, shrewd business women or good parents. They would hope that they will have enough money to send their children to college or to make their children's lives a little better than their own. The sign of hope is when we see some of these things coming to fruition. We work to make these things happen.

We hope for many things in our lives. We pray and hope that we will get to heaven. We all know what we have to do to get there, very simple, love God with all our hearts and our neighbor as ourselves, not easy but a mandate given to us by Jesus Himself. Today there are many fears that make us hope. We hope for peace, joy, security, more money and prestige. Sometimes we hope for things that make no sense to others but makes plenty sense to us. Hope, you say, is just another word for wishing, but actually it is trust in God; that what we hope for will be realized.

Sometimes when we hope for things and they do not come to fruition we tend to lose hope. But there are always signs of hope if we put our trust and sights on God. Nothing is impossible with God. Even when things go terribly wrong there is still hope. God does not work in accidents. Even when things do not seem to work out, there is still hope. When God seems to forget about us that is when we really put our hope in Him. Even if God takes a loved one or our money, all is not lost; we know that God does all things for our good even when they look bad. We turn our live over to God and keep on hoping and believing in Him. God knows all our thoughts, our needs, our wants and even our greed. God wants us to turn to him and put our hope in Him. God is our sign of hope.

When people have great tragedy in their lives they are sadden but do not lose hope. You see this sign of hope when we see them empathizing with one another, helping each other get through the terror like what happened at Columbine, Virginia Tech, Nine Eleven, earthquakes around the world and especially the one in Haiti, Tsunami and the tragedy in the theatre showing the movie *Batman* in Aurora, Colorado. In any tragedy people will rally around the victims and try to do whatever they can to assuage their suffering. People who survive these tragedies are very flexible and able to bounce back because they have such faith and hope in their lives. They are able to reach out to the wider community. People all over the world seek for signs of hope in their lives.

In spite of evil we can still make this world a better place, one place at a time. We do need to know that God is with us in all of our tragedies.

We look at our country and see all the senseless killings, the racism, the dishonesty and human trafficking… all this evil that is going on around us and still there are signs of hope. The hope is in our belief in a just and merciful God as we try to do our part in the process. We know that God is there to help us out of our trials and troubles if we need Him. We can walk and not grow weary. We must wait on the Lord ... lean on God. Sometimes, it seems as if God is away and will never come back… but by and by… we see Him working in our lives when we turn to Him in hope. God loves us so much that He sent His Son Jesus to die for us. So God will never ever leave us. God will never abandon us.

SIGNS OF HOPE IN BIBLICAL TIMES

Look at Job, how God took everything from him, everything… material wealth, children. Yet Job hoped and believed in God. God rewarded Job's faith and hope and restored all he had lost. Joseph was thrown in jail because he was falsely accused but he had hope in God and this hope was rewarded. He became a great man in the life of Egypt and saved the lives of many … the Egyptians, his own people and others.

In (Matthew 9:18-25) we see the woman with the issue of blood, she hoped that Jesus would heal her, she did not just wish it she did something about it. She reached out her hand and touched Jesus. In the same story we have the ruler Jarius who had a very sick daughter who later died. Because of his hope in Jesus' ability to be able to do all things, led to the raising of his daughter from death to life. He could have despaired but no, he sought Jesus. We can look at the Syo-Phonician woman who asked Jesus to heal her daughter who was possessed by a demon. She was insulted by Jesus' saying we do not give our children's food to the dogs. Her reply was so classic, "But even the dogs eat the crumbs that drops from the table." Jesus marveled at her faith and hope and cured her daughter. Ten Lepers approached Jesus for a cure. They could have been afraid to approach Jesus but no there they were, asking Jesus to heal them. All were healed. All these people hoped in Jesus and their hope and trust were rewarded.

Signs of hope were seen at the end of slavery. Especially through the work of the Abolitionist Movement and other courageous men and women like Harriet Tubman, Harriet Beecher Stowe. Hope is seen at the eradication of Jim Crow through the efforts of fearless men and women prior to and up to Rosa Parks, Martin Luther King Jr. and others. Racism is not dead but there is hope that through the efforts of many, this too will pass. Just as these people hoped and believed so we too can do the same. We can take back our streets and our children… one... at a time by paying attention to them, giving them the love that they need and praying for them. Sometimes they will stray but we need to be there to love them back to life. God never gives up on us so we must never give up on God or each other. God does expect us to help ourselves by getting involved at all level in our society; we must get involved in our governing process at the local level as well as the national level. When we do our part God will do his part. For God is our only hope in a constantly changing and seemingly evil world.

Signs of hope can be seen in senior citizens helping the young to read and to learn other skills. It is people working together making our communities better. Priest, Sisters, Brothers, Deacons and Lay Ministers work to bring Christ to the poor, young and elderly. We see hope in doctors taking their vacation time to go to Third World countries to minister to the sick. Others also do the same in their spare time. I am sure you who are reading this can think of others who bring hope to the world at large. It is great seeing people helping people in the name of God.

Saint Paul speaks about hope in the context of the virtues of faith and love. (I Cor. 13:13) "*There abide faith hope and love but the greater of these virtues is love*" Hope will disappear faith will be accomplished when we die and see God face to face. But it is love which will last when all is past, for we will have gained our mission in life. For all eternity we will love God, we will not have need for faith for our yearning has been accomplished and our hope realized. There is always hope until we meet the Lord. Let us never give up hope.

SYMBOLS OF HOPE

THE CROSS ---- THE BIBLE ---- THE RAINBOW ---- THE DOVE ---- THE EGG

THE BUTTERFLY --- THE ANCHOR ---- LIGHT IN THE DARK

I read something on the internet one day that said, ***"Don't worry about tomorrow...God is already there.*"** In our convent we have a banner that says, "***Providence rises before the sun."*** Let us continue to see a sign of hope in the world for God has us all in the Palm of His Hand.

May God bless us...and let us be signs of hope to one another, in our homes, schools, business, work places, our church and our world!

CHAPTER 8

Personal Holiness

Spiritual formation is ongoing and must be intentional. Unless we give our spiritual life priority we will never gain that level of holiness or spiritual connection with Jesus that we had in our first fervor. So when we intentionally make our lives relevant and centered on Biblical teaching, Spiritual Reading, Meditation of all kinds and types, we will find that our lives will be full and more meaningful.

We will look at our spiritual life in a different light. We will look our neighbor differently; our driving habits will no longer be the same for we will be tolerant of other drivers... we will look at our neighbor, who gets on our last nerve, in a new and positive way. We will look at the beggar, the dope addict and other derelicts in the light of Christ; looking them in the eye, speaking to them and not crossing the street to avoid contact with them.

Being intentional in our prayer life and daily living, we will see a vast change in our attitude towards God in prayer and our neighbor as we rub shoulders each day. Our whole day will be a meditation as we strive to eradicate evil thoughts about our neighbor, rash judging or how to get even. We know about getting even. Someone does something real or imagine… we will get them. You know all these little evil things we harbor in our minds if we are not intentional in our thoughts, words or actions. It is not easy but will become easier as we practice. It is said that practice makes perfect. God calls all of us to personal holiness.

Religious are not the only ones who need to be intentional, for God calls all baptized persons to holiness. Being intentional can change our lives. This is the kind of thinking and acting that will led us to a personal relationship with Christ as we travel to the Kingdom.

Surface living is not an option, for anyone who has given themselves to God, be they religious or lay. Intentional living gives us the opportunity to work out our salvation in an atmosphere of serene dependence on God; knowing that whatever we do is for the love of God. Intentional living keeps us centered in Christ and neighbor focused without irritation and resentment for having to be all thing to all peoples. Intentional living cost us nothing, except being focused. If we focus on pleasing God we will always keep Him in mind when we are tempted to dislike or hate our neighbor for intended wrongs or unintended faults.

Intentional living is simply living a simple life like Jesus. Settling things as they arise and living each day as if it will be the last day of our lives. It is always keeping God in our sight.

Following Jesus

The Apostles left everything to follow Jesus. At the beginning of the ministry of Jesus, asked by two of the Apostles where he lived, Jesus replied, "Come and you will see." (John 1: 38-39) others followed. They never looked back. Yes they were argumentative, yes they were looking for worldly gains, and yes they all ran away when Jesus needed them most. We have to realize that they were human, poor fishermen with little or no education. But are we any different than they when it comes to being always faithful to Jesus? We sometimes act like these poor fishermen of Galilee.

As I contemplate the invitation of Jesus to the Apostles, to come and see; I reflect on my own call to follow Jesus at the tender age of five. Still answering the call eighty some years later, means saying yes everyday to that invitation to, come and see. Being called to ministry is serious business, a serious commitment. Each day is a recommitment to that call; indeed every minute of every day is a yes.

Answering the call of Jesus, no matter what state of life we profess, requires commitment. It means being able to look the addict, the alcoholic, the prostitute, the beggar, and indeed all of God's children in the eye. We have to realize that we are all precious in the eyes of God. It takes perseverance. It takes love and practice to see others as God sees them.

Being a follower of Christ means we have to be AVAILABLE, in season and out of season. Availability is an everyday thing. Not only when we "FEEL GOOD" or on "CLOUD NINE" but those times when all we want to do is be alone and be left alone. These are the times when the, "Come and see" really mean "come and see." We see Jesus where we are in good times as well as adverse circumstances. Being a follower of Jesus is not easy. It demands sacrifice, self-abasement and abandonment to Divine Providence.

This means that in whatever situation we find ourselves there is the Trinity to lend a helping hand. Jesus was very careful to make sure that we were not alone in our work for the Kingdom. He sent the Holy Spirit to assist us in all the works of the Lord. The Holy Spirit enables us to continue to "come and see." To be called by Jesus is no accident. God does not work in accidents; it is pure grace from God and must be taken seriously.

An Opportunity of a Lifetime

What is this "Opportunity of a Lifetime?" Every day we live is an "Opportunity of a Lifetime" situation. God gives us the opportunity each day to praise him one more time one way or the other. Each action that we perform daily is an opportunity. It is said that we will never have the same day twice. When the day is over, it is over, never to be repeated. So, therefore, we can truly say this… that every day is, *"An Opportunity of a Lifetime."*

As Christians, we know that there are no accidents in life only certainties. As we walk this journey of life let us look at all the graces given to us throughout our lives. These opportunities are ours to use and to cooperate with the plan of God.

What is God's plan for my life? Each day affords you and me the opportunity to find the answer through discerning reflective prayer. Ask Jesus to open your mind, heart and soul to the promptings of the blessed Holy Spirit who will lead and guide you. Leave all your worries and cares in God's capable hands. Allow yourself to be washed in the grace and love of our good and gracious God. Seize the moment. Each day is an opportunity to become a better person. Things around us try to drag us under their spell, to distract us from what is really important. But if we are focused on Jesus we will not let the opportunity to do better, pass us by. We will learn to be carriers of the torch of peace and justice to our world.

People who do not know Jesus, will go to any length to seek out opportunities that will further their careers. This has nothing to do with religion. They do it purely on the natural level. What a lesson for us who know who Jesus is and who follow Jesus. This knowledge can catapult us to a deeper union with Jesus, to become Jesus to others.

CHAPTER 9

Life and Relationships

Life is not about acquiring things. It is about getting to know God by the practice of virtue. Just as we become what we receive each day in Holy Communion so we must become other Christ's for the world. Imitating Christ cannot be done simply by wishing it; an action has to take place. The life of Christ in us must become part and parcel of our every day activities.

More effort has to be put forth in our daily meditation as well as other forms of prayer. Our Baptism calls all of us to strive for personal holiness. We cannot become holy unless we work at it. We cannot sit in front of the TV all day long, read all kinds of novels or engage in other mundane things and expect to become holy. We have to continually have our eyes fixed on Jesus. Jesus is our answer to ward off worldly distractions, worldly desires. All of these tendencies are our enemies. These needs and wants have to be torn out, torn out through prayer and sacrifice.

We are all called to holiness of life. Therefore we have to do violence to ourselves. The body wants what it wants so doing violence to our senses will help us achieve our goal. This goal is a personal relationship with Jesus. We must form a personal relationship with Jesus. What does that mean? It means we walk and talk with Jesus and take Him as our best friend, someone we turn to talk intimately with; being able to tell him our most intimate thoughts. He knows them anyway but loves to have us repeat our wants and needs. Jesus loves to have us ask for help and to talk to Him like a friend without begging for anything just talking; as the Spanish people would say, "Hablar por hablar," "talking just to be talking." We can do that, "Can't we?"

We are the Church…

The Body of Christ

We are the Church, we represent Christ here on earth and we are privileged to receive Christ each day in the Eucharist. How has this daily reception of the Eucharist changed my outlook, my attitudes? Am I my same old self? What in me needs to change?

Sometimes we operate on a purely natural plane… so how has this daily "Encounter" with my Eucharistic Lord changed my outlook in my life and those lives I touch daily? How does it challenge me, a member of the Church, a part of the Body of Christ?

Help Me

Lord, help me see me
As you see me.
Let me die to self
So that others will see
Only you in me.
Help me to become
What I receive each day.

Short prayer before the Blessed Sacrament

Lord God, I bow before you in humble adoration. I know that you are truly present, body and soul in the tabernacle of this altar. I beg you to give me strength to serve you as I should. As I meet each person every day let me see You, Jesus, in them and let them see You, Jesus, in me. Amen.

And the Word Became Flesh

When the "Word" is implanted in my heart and my being acts upon this "Word" the process of personal commitment begins. God was so good to us He sent the Word into the world. My responsibility is to respond to the Word in a positive manner. To respond I must open my heart and mind to the teaching of the Word who dwelt among us.

Hanging on to the teachings of the Word, my world of "self" will have to change. I will have to change. I will have to become all things to all peoples. To become a "Christ Bearer" my focus must be that of Christ in all aspect of my life. How am I doing in this regard?

A

"A Monstrance for Christ"

We speak of Eucharistic Adoration as if it is the only way we can adore Christ in the Eucharist. It is said that we are all Eucharistic people simply by the fact that we receive Jesus each day in the sacrament of the Eucharist. This, in itself, makes us all a pix, for we each carry Jesus in our souls, which is then carried about in this body of ours for all to see...not only for others to see but for others to emulate. Receiving Jesus each day is an awesome responsibility.

The body then, is the Monstrance. We are holy people, who sometimes act badly, which do not necessarily make us bad people. We can all become better if we remember who we are and "WHO" it is we are carrying about within our souls daily. To be able to do any of this we must pray for the strength to be able to do these things.

It is not easy but will become so with practice. Any skill that we wish to learn need practice. Anyone in serious sports will tell you that they must practice for hours to get their particular skill perfected. So too with the spiritual life, it must be worked at daily. Heaven is worth that and more.

IS YOUR COMMUNION HOLY?

Because we go to Holy Communion on a daily basic, we have a tendency to be a bit caviler or nonchalant in our reception of this great and holy sacrament. This is not a condemnation of anyone, but frequency sometimes brings on a common attitude, not so much contempt, for we would not do that to the Lord, but an air of familiarity thus making us take the Eucharist for granted.

We know how much Saint Paul talked about people receiving communion without much reverence or thought. We certainly do not want to be counted in that number. We cannot make a proper thanksgiving to the Lord after receiving His Sacred Body to eat and His Precious Blood to drink by then rushing out the door with Him is our mouths. As Christians we have a duty to give the Lord our utter most respect. We talk about others but are we doing the same thing? As christians, our respect for the Eucharist should surpass that of others who do not have our understanding of the Sacrificial offering of Jesus daily on our altars.

B

Eucharistic Reflections

There is so much we can pray and ask Jesus for as we kneel before the tabernacle each day or each week. We do need to ask Jesus for what we need, like concerns for our world, the Church, our family and friends. Sometimes, it seems that there is no time for personal prayer and reflection.

We need to take time, "TO JUST BE." To be with Jesus in the Blessed Sacrament letting our minds steep itself in the Divine Presence. It does not matter if the mind wanders because Jesus knows that you are there and want to be there. Just your presence is enough for Him. It does not matter if the head nods or the eyes close for a while or even if there is a snore now and then. Jesus accepts your intention of just being there.

We have to give God the chance of being God. God sees our intentions and that is all that matters. We give honor and praise to God each time we receive the Body and Blood of the Lord. We go to the doctor all through the year to stay healthy, taking care of our bodies. Are not our souls worth the year round reverence we must cultivate for our souls?

Familiarity is not an option when we talk about the Eucharist in our lives. If we want to become holy, it can happen through our devotion to Jesus in the Eucharist. If we become what we receive each day, as we say we do, then our only option is personal holiness. And that is what God is calling all of us to, personal holiness. This means having a personal relationship with Christ so that we can be that perfect person God calls each of us to become.

This personal holiness comes, first of all, as baptized Christians or as religious, through the Eucharist. Secondly, our consciences call us to it, our Church calls us to it, and the world calls us to it simply by our baptism as followers of Christ.

Feed Me Lord

Give me Lord each day
Your body to eat
And your blood to drink.

Food for now and tomorrow
Food for the journey
We must take in the end.

The Eucharist is Serious Business

As we begin each day to contemplate the days in life as members of the Mystical Body of Christ we cannot help but think about the thoughtfulness of Jesus. Only a loving God would think to have his children feed daily on him to become food for his children. Yet that is what we do day after day, after day, feed on Jesus. Yet, we act as if this is some ordinary bread and ordinary wine that we feel we need to have each day to save face or because we are there... so we go receive. Communion is not to become a casual occurrence in our lives.

Christ did not intend this reception of his Body and Blood to be a casual occurrence. No, it was for us to become other Christ to build up the Body of Christ. Our home is where this action must take place first. We then allow this love to spill over into our interaction with others with whom we meet. Each day is an encounter with Jesus. Each time we meet any sister or brother is as encounter with Jesus.

Being a Christian calls us to bring Christ to all we meet, this is a mandate that we cannot avoid for we are bread and wine to each other. We have to become what we receive; our very salvation depends on it.

The Eucharistic Liturgy is considered the most important part of our Catholic faith life. In union with Jesus, the Father works through us, to bring us to that perfect person through the Eucharistic. The Word and Eucharistic Liturgy unite us fully with the Trinity. This union fortifies our souls to continue this hypostatic union with all whom we meet. Since we receive Jesus at Holy Communion, we become another Christ, thus whenever anyone encounters us they really and truly encounters Jesus. Think about it!

The Holy Spirit

Allegany Arts

Jesus told the Apostle to be strong and not be afraid, that He would send the Holy Spirit upon them. That the Holy Spirit would be with them always, to guide them in all that they need for the furthering of the Kingdom, for spreading the gospel.

Jesus did not just promise this to the Apostles and Disciples of long ago but to us today. We are the Church and are all filled with the Holy Spirit. This happens at our Baptism and in a very special way at our Confirmation.

As Christians we know that without the Guidance of the Holy Spirit that the Church could not survive. We tend to forget the Holy Spirit, but it is the Spirit who sanctifies and leads the Church through difficult times. It is the fire that keeps thing burning brightly.

Scripture and the Church tell us that the Holy Spirit is the Advocate of the Body of Christ. She is the one who continues to sanctify and keep the fire of Jesus burning in our hearts, minds and souls. This is the Person of the Trinity who will be with us to the end of the world. She is our intercessor and mouth piece, as it were to the Father and the Son. We sometimes forget that it is the Holy Spirit that Jesus promised would be with us to complete the teachings that were begun by Him. Isn't it wonderful to know that we have such a person right at our fingertip to make intercession for us?

Come, O Holy Spirit and fill the hearts
of the faithful and enkindle in our hearts
the "FIRE" of your love.

*L*ed by the Spirit in Peace

Led by the Spirit, we are called to live in peace. This brings to mind the total message of Jesus. When Jesus was born in Bethlehem, the Angels told the Shepherd that they were bringing them good news of great joy. This joy was Jesus, the Prince of Peace.

The whole life of Jesus was about peace. Just before Jesus went up to heaven He gave the Apostles His peace. Not only peace to the Apostles but to us as well. Jesus promised to send the Holy Spirit to them to solidify that covenant that began so long ago in Bethlehem.

At Pentecost the Spirit became visible, no longer was the Spirit a word, or a myth but a reality. Today, we claim that peace brought forth by the Spirit through our Baptism, Confirmation and again in our ministry to the people of God.

To God Be the Glory

To God be the glory
For all the things
He has done for me.

Good thing
And not so good things,
But all these happenings
Worked for my good.

He made waves for me,
Then crooked path
He made straight.

My bad times
Became good times...
Because of God's
Great grace, love and mercy…

I can truly say
Deep in my heart
To God be the glory

With the Holy Spirit
To guide our way
Everything we do
Is holy.

HOLY DAYS

AND

HOLIDAYS

CHAPTER 10

Thanksgiving Is Everyday

There is a song entitled, "Every Day is a Day of Thanksgiving." Yes, every day truly is a "Day of Thanksgiving" every day we must give thanks and praise to God not only for food, family, relatives, clothing and friends but for allowing us see another day, and for the whole of creation. We hear so much about Global warming and how this knowledge is impacting the world and will impact future generations yet unborn.

This and every Thanksgiving Day let us lift our eyes to heaven and ask pardon for our unwise use of the great gifts that were given to our care. To resolve to be frugal in the use of water and other natural resources that we take so much for granted.

Thanksgiving is also a time to think of people less fortunate than we, to remember them in prayer as well as contributions if possible. It must be very hard for a mother to see her child die of starvation when there is so much food wasted daily.

Our prayer on Thanksgiving Day may be one in which we ask God to provide food for those who have none and to open the hearts of peoples of the world to be generous at home and abroad.

That one day, poverty will be wiped from the face of the earth and all of God's children will be well fed and clothed. Every day is truly a Day of Thanksgiving, for God has been so good to us. He keeps on blessing us and we give thanks and heart-felt praise. Amen and Amen.

We Give Thanks

We give thanks to God
For all the goods of the earth
Our plants and bright sun too.

We give thanks to God
For every nation and race
Who live on this great land.

We give thanks to God
For Moms, Dads, children
Plus technology too.

We give thanks to God
For churches, food and good schools
And courage to love each other.

We give thanks to God
For all his many blessings
Lord, we give you thanks.

Advent Preparation

"Prepare the way of the Lord," was the cry of John the Baptist on the bank of the Jordan River. That is what Advent is, a means of preparation for the coming of the Savior, Jesus Christ. We get so busy trying to prepare for Christmas with cleaning, cooking, and gift getting that we lose sight of this wonderful season.

Contemplating Christmas is a walk with Mary as she contemplated the birth of her first born Son. Her whole day was filled with the thoughts of the blessed event. So, too, our thoughts must be focused on the coming Savior.

Advent allows us time to think and plan for our future … eternity. We are able to get in touch with our own sinfulness in whatever form that may take. Sometimes it takes a season like this for us to face our own demons and rectify our lives and design them according to the dictates of God.

Advent is that time of year when we see autumn winding down in preparation for winter. The leaves on the trees have almost all fallen off and the harvest is done or almost done. People are celebrating the special feast of Thanksgiving for all that God has done for us from this time last year to the present. We thank God for family friends, yes and enemies too, for all are God's children whether we want to admit that or not.

We look at the Thanksgiving holiday as a new beginning, so it is with our celebration of Advent. It is a new beginning. For St. John says in John 1:1 "In the beginning was the Word and the Word was God." Not only is it a time to give thanks for harvest and everything that is connected with the thought, but foremost we give thanks that Jesus said yes to the request of the Father. This Advent or "coming" is what Advent is all about, a setting free, a change, and a metanoia. When we say "O Come, O Come Emmanuel" this year, let us really mean it. Come, Lord Jesus, Come.

Our prayer could be thus…

Lord Jesus, you know the thoughts that are in the deepest recesses of our hearts. Pluck from these poor weak hearts of ours all that is not of you and give us the courage to continue this conversion long after Advent has ceased. You, O Lord, are the giver of all good gifts and we know that you answer all prayers in your own time and fashion. We ask this prayer as we ask all things from your goodness and bounty. Amen

Christmas… A Time for Love

Allegany Arts

Christmas they say is a time for love, and so it is. Why, because Christ who is love became human for our sake. What is that but love? Who in their right mind would leave heaven to come down to earth to save people who really did not want to be saved? People who want to do their own will and insist on going about their business seeking their own agendas. We thumb our noses at God as it were, not paying God at times, no respect at all.

Are we Christians exempt from the above observations? Do we really understand the ramification of the debt we owe to Jesus for saying yes to the Father by coming to earth as a baby to ultimately give his life for the sins of us all? Let us reflect on this love of Jesus, this totally giving of self for us and rethink our priorities.

Christmas is a time to remember others by prayers, and by engaging in almsgiving and financial assistance. Each day we need to spread the blessings as we remember all the blessings that God has given us and spread them to our sisters and brothers.

Christmas is Every Day of the Year

Have you ever thought about Christmas being a year round daily celebration? Yet, that is what it is, a year round celebration from December to December. Christmas is a daily living concept in the same way as when Christ was born in Bethlehem. Christmas you say comes once a year. It comes and goes but does it? The celebration has ceased outwardly but Christmas is with us daily. Each day the Word becomes flesh at the Eucharistic Celebration all over the world wherever the Eucharistic Liturgy is celebrated.

We become so used to the Eucharistic Liturgy that it becomes routine and common place, but this Jesus, born in a manger over 2000 years ago to the Blessed Virgin Mary, is there with us each and every day. Every day the Word becomes flesh and lives among us. Each day is a "Come let us adore Him" moment. Let this thought fill our spirits as we enter into the mystery of the Incarnation… again…and again with "O Come let us adore Him, Christ the Lord."

Oh
Come let us adore Him
Christ the Lord.

The New Year
A New Beginning

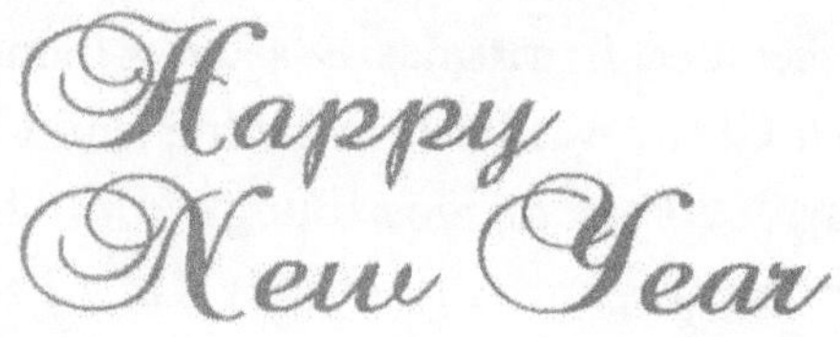

Each year God gives us the opportunity to begin anew. We have the opportunity to become better people and make our world, community, homes and work places fitting places to live and operate. We are afforded the pleasure of making things right with our God, our families and ourselves. The New Year is not so much about making resolutions, which most of us break anyway, but to become better people. In becoming better people, we can do all those things we resolved to do.

The New Year allows us to take inventory of our lives from the past year and gives us the opportunity to begin afresh if our lives were not what we thought it should have been. It is the year of the "Second Chance," as it were. Another chance to get it right, whatever the right is, for each person. The New Year allows us to say, "I am sorry Lord, for messing up, help me to do better in this New Year." Or it could act as the impetus to catapult us into doing that special thing we have been putting off doing. We should all thank God for a New Year, a new beginning.

We thank God for all His graces and blessings from last year until now especially for the gift of life, family, and friends and just for making it to another New Year. We might say that the New Year is a year of Thanksgiving. Thus we have two Thanksgiving Holidays, one in November and another in January. We thank God for the good, the bad and the indifferent. We give thanks, honor and praise to God for all his many blessings.

New Year Reflections

How can one properly thank God?
In ways that is fitting,
Because God is God …and
There is no other as good as God.

Yet, God wants us to be thankful.
Not from a sense of guilt,
Because God is God…and
There is no other as good as God.

God loves you, all the world, and me
For God is our friend in need and deed.
Because God is God …and
There is no other as good as God.

Each New Year we thank God,
We thank God for another year of living.
For another year to praise and give thanks.
Because God is God…and
There is no other as good as God.

Thank you God, the God of New Years,
The God of New Years long past
And New Years yet to come
Because God is God…and
There is no other as good as God.

Celebration of Lent

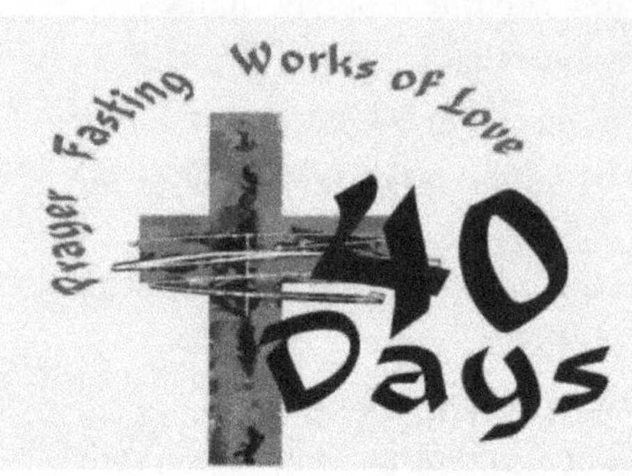

As we contemplate and reflect on the debt that Christ paid for our sin we reflect on the Season of Lent. Lent is not a time for grown-ups to give up candy but a time of true spiritual growth by looking at our daily sinfulness and reflect on how we can grow in true holiness.

Holiness is not a pie in the sky concept, but growth in the love of Jesus and the neighbor. It is a metanoia, a change of heart, a spiritual awareness. It is getting a real relationship with Jesus through reading of Sacred Scripture, daily spiritual reading and getting in touch with ourselves. It is being patient with us, our brothers and sisters in Christ.

Lent is a time to read your Bible and *meditate* on how we can become better people. As we meditate on what we have read in the Bible our hearts begin to change and we become different people. We give to charity and if time permits, volunteer at Youth Centers, give to charity and perform other charitable services.

What does Lent hold for me?

What will Jesus exact from us during the season of lent? Lent is a time to reflect on how we have cooperated with God's graces from the last lent to this lent. If things did not measure up to what we thought God wanted from us then this year we need to pay extra attention to the workings of the Holy Spirit in our lives.

Lent is not just about giving up things, it is also about getting something and being more present to Jesus and ultimately to others in our lives. We have to begin to live above the mundane level of daily living. As Christians we are expected to do more than give up candy but to look at those areas in our lives that are **not life-giving** for ourselves or for those with whom we live.

Living on a purely natural level must not be a part of our lives as people of God who have dedicated their lives to God through our baptismal promises made through our Godparents and confirmation, which we made of our own free will and volition. Confirmation makes us adult Christians and we must be about doing adult things. No one can do for us what we can do for ourselves. No day in our lives should be the **"USUAL."** Our striving for personal holiness goes beyond the usual and takes on the action of Christ who did the **"UNUSUAL"** by dying on the cross for us one **"SAD, SAD"** Friday afternoon on a hill called **Calvary**. Our Redemption was won on a tree… on a hill … made sacred by the blood of Jesus Christ. Can we not be the best we can be for the sake of the Kingdom?

Alleluia, Alleluia, Alleluia
The Lord has truly risen …
Alleluia, Alleluia

Easter is a **Holy Day,** a day of great rejoicing with plenty of Alleluias. Easter and Christmas are two great holidays, but it is Easter that really connects us to the Father, Son and Holy Spirit. We might say that Easter is the glue that binds together all the pieces that were not connected at Christmas. Easter completes the puzzle. It connects the Old Testament prophesies and begins the New Order of things. Easter chronicled the stories and passed them to us in the coming of the Holy Spirit who will, as Jesus told us in no uncertain term. It is the Holy Spirit who will be with us until Jesus comes again to judge the world. Now we have a straight path to God. We do not need a messenger who will take our messages to the very throne of God, no mediation as in the Old Testament.

Through the death and resurrection of Jesus we can go immediately to God himself and ask for anything we want. We can talk to the Father, Son or Spirit in a very personal way. Isn't that wonderful, that we are free to approach the very throne of God? As the children would say... that is so awesomely cool.

Jesus rose triumphantly from the grave and by his rising we are able to rise to the throne of God. We can become other Christ to our sisters and brothers. We can become imitators of Jesus. We do not have to stay in our sins.

Through the life and death of Jesus we can rise to new heights. We can be like Jesus, carrying him throughout the places we frequent day by day. Not in a showy manner but as humble servants of the humble Master.

Easter Hallelujahs

Easter, a time to fill the earth with Hallelujah trills
Recalling anew the Master's dearly beloved Son
Dying for us one Friday on Calvary's lonely hill
Paying the ultimate price… our salvation He won.

To heaven we can prepare happily to go,
To sing God's praises of joyful heartfelt thanks
For the sacrifice Christ whose love did show,
Allowing human-kind to join the angelic ranks.

Hallelujahs resound sweetly all around
As we sing our own heavenly Hallelujah song.
Thanking God with soulful melodious sounds,
Of Hallelujah, Hallelujah all the day long.

Easter is a preparation for heaven… seems strange
But we'll meet family and many good friends.
There we will meet and greet Mother Mary Lange,
As we sing Hallelujah, Hallelujah without end.

MEMORIAL DAY

Every year we celebrate Memorial Day. Memorial Day is really a day of thanksgiving. A day to give thank to God for our freedom. A day to appreciate and pray for the men and women in the Armed Forces living and deceased who have given their lives so that we, in these United States of America might be free from all harm and danger.

We remember in a special way those women and men who have given their lives in the present conflict in Iraq, Afghanistan and other parts of the world. We pray for the relatives and friends of those who are grieving for their dead. We pray for those who will continue to die so that we all might all indeed be free.

As Christians, we believe that Jesus is the Resurrection and the Life and that all who die will be united with him in glory and will rise again on the last day. Let us rejoice in this great love of our God for us,

SHIFTING GEARS

CHAPTER 11

AIDS/HIV... and African American Women

AIDS/HIV as it affects the African American population is out of proportion. Many think that there is no such monster among the African American Community. Wrong! It is said that the proportion of aids among African American women is alarming. It is reported that 20 percent of women who have AIDS/HIV are intravenous users and share needles. Another way that AIDS/HIV is transmitted is through unprotected sexual activity and lastly from husbands or boyfriends. African American males have the habit of having sexual relations with both heterosexual and homosexual persons with no protection and bring the disease home. Children born to these affected women will be without parents and many will have do have the AIDS/HIV virus themselves

One of the drawbacks on the story of AIDS/HIV virus is the lack of information in the Black and Hispanic Community. Children as young as the elementary grades, high school and collages need to have some serious education about this dreaded disease. Many politicians are not too concerned because the epidemic has not affected the white community in the same proportion as it has affected the Black and Hispanic Communities.

AIDS/HIV is so wide spread because of ignorance. Much of this disease can be eradicated through education. As a country we need to take our heads out of the sand and look at this Aids epidemic for what it is, a deadly disease, and a killer.

Looking at a chart on the Internet concerning AIDS/HIV the rate for African Americans who have contracted the disease is 75.2 %, Hispanics 26.8 %, American Indian 10.4 %, White 7.2 % and Asian/ Pacific Islander 4.8 %. What does that say to the Black Community? We have work to do.

Globally there are 37.8 million or more adults and children living with the HIV/AIDS. Most of them were living in low and middle-income countries. We are supposed to be in a better place but statistically the African American community is in bad straits. The sad part about all this is that there are more African American women affected than men.

It is said that the AIDS epidemic in the United States among African Americans is equal to that of the Third World especially South Africa. Parents need to read about Aids and the harm that it can bring to one's family members. Lack of knowledge and understanding help spread the AIDS/HIV virus. Young men and women must be taught to take greater responsibility for their action. The ideal is sexual abstinence. Condoms are not a safe means of protection.

The definition for AIDS is Acquired Immunodeficiency Syndrome. It is a virus, which attacks the immune system. It was first reported in the United States in 1981 and has since become a worldwide epidemic. It is caused by the human immunodeficiency virus (HIV), because it kills or damages body cells of the immune system; it is hard for the body to build up cells to fight the disease and certain cancers. Since there is no certain cure for the disease it overtakes the immune system and eats away at the body.

Before AIDS was thought to be so contagious it was a possibility that a person who was ill and given tainted blood by way of a blood transfusion could contact the disease. Arthur Ashe was a good example of someone contracting AIDS through a blood transfusion. However, the medical community has devised ways of screening blood from everyone who donates blood. Now it is relatively safe to have a blood transfusion and not be afraid of contracting the AIDS/HIV virus.

What are the implications for our Religious Education Programs and other related Services? We have the duty to teach AIDS education as part of our curriculum as well as the Public Schools. AIDS does not discriminate; it affects Catholics as well as anyone else. AIDS/HIV is a deadly disease. We in the African American community need to take steps to save our people. AIDS education and awareness is up to us and no one else. Our bad habits must change. Are we up to the challenge?

Many think that because the Aids epidemic seemingly is over there are no reasons to be careful and continue to make people aware of the disease. This is a disease that will linger and we all need to be aware of its lethal effect on our lives and the lives of the people we care about. It is something that we must pray about and change our behavior.

It is only through prayer and education that this dreaded disease can be wiped out along with treatment. It reminds me of leprosy in the time of Christ. In ancient times lepers had to shout, unclean, unclean whenever they came into contact with other people. I do not advocate doing that in these modern times but I do advocate that anyone who has Aids that they warn their partner and get treatment.

CHAPTER 12

Africans, Who Became African Americans

Who are we?

Many of us do not want to shoulder the concept that we as African, now known as African Americans, who came from Africa as slaves. True, there are black people all over the world and yes; all of them have roots from Africa. Like it or not Black people are the products of Mother Africa. Everyone talks wars, the treatment of each other. Where was the Church when black men, the black women and black children were dragged from their homes, uprooted to work in the cotton field and elsewhere as non-human or a certain percent human to work as slave . . . and being told that you had no souls. If you make people believe that they have no worth, thus brainwashing them to think after a fashion to believe that you were only fit to work from sunset to sundown, then you have no problem making these people do whatever they were told.

No vigil was held for these hapless slaves. This was the state of America before the Civil War. But then, there has been slavery throughout the world but America took the prize as being the cruelest captors with their slaves.

We often hear people say that we have to stop thinking about slavery that we are in America now and are Americans. And so we are. But Africa is our Homeland and a people who do not know where they came from cannot possibly know where they are going. Other Ethnic groups are always talking about their roots, their heritage. Well Black people have roots and a heritage as well and should not be ashamed of our "Blackness." Alex Haley showed us that in **Roots**. So why are there denial and the tendency to hold back and deny our history? Do we want to be a people who have no past, no present and no future? Or do we want to be a people who are proud of our black ancestry and homeland? Even today white people think that blacks are expendable. Yet, the majority of blacks and whites both profess a belief and say they serve the same God. Sometime one has to wonder if some white people still think that black people are only fit to be slaves or in these modern times. only fit to do menial tasks and still have no souls. Some people forget that Jesus came on earth to redeem all humankind; that with God, there is no partiality.

Although we have a painful past we must embrace that past and build upon it, not deny it. Sometimes we spend so much time denying our African Roots and trying to be someone else that we tend to stand still in time while other ethnic groups are forging forward. Although some of us were slaves here in America, it was and is a past reality but we should work toward building a secure future. We must remember that Africa has a rich past before it was raped by Europe of our finest men, women and children. Our Ancestors were Kings and Queens. We have a rich history of which we should be proud.

Our black men and women, and yes some white men and women have fought long and hard to make America free for all. However, because of much ignorance on the part of some, to keep the status quo, we are sometimes intimidated. Many say we are a forgiving people and so we are but we should not allow this tendency to make us soft and not continue to strive for total equality. We must not get weary and discouraged and think, what's the use! Yet others have trudged on like the Negro National Anthem says, "God of our weary years God of our silent tears, Thou Who has brought us thus far on our way."

African Americans built this country with its slave labor and long after slavery ended we toiled long and hard to gain acceptance as citizens of this country. Yet we still see the ugly face of racism raise its head now and again to say to the Black man and Black woman you have not yet arrived. How is this true?

Look at our school systems, usually we are given the worst teachers, very little funding, hand-me down books and poor run-down buildings. Very seldom is there a school built just for us. We are the last hired and the first fired. We go into a bank for a loan and spend days and months wrangling with the bank officials to complete the transaction. Our black men live on the edge with white policemen harassing them by pulling them over because they are in an expensive car or they think they must be dealing in drugs. There is a saying that, "Black people are harassed and arrested while driving black" in America.

Why am I writing this? I guess it has been in my head for a long time and this is venting time. It is not that we hate white people because it is not all white people who give blacks a hard time but there are enough in these United States to make our lives quite uncomfortable. However, with the grace of God, "We Shall Overcome some day" as the song of the Civil Rights Movement says. Then, too, because we are all children of God we are all sisters and brothers and so must love each sister or brother and pray for those who believe that God has a preference. A good Father loves all his children equally.

However, when we think there is an equalizing force, here comes some racist, to begin the turmoil all over again. This gives other well-meaning white people a bad name. Yet people will say to us, get over this slavery business but it is just because of this slavery business, this past history that we cannot live in peace. I say to those who do not like people of color, to get over it, we are here to stay. If enough bigots got over their hatred then this world would be a much better place for all concerned.

Let me say again, that we helped build these United States with our blood, sweat and tears. We are here for the long haul. I say like the Jews say of Israel, "God brought us to this land and gave it to us." So it is with Blacks, Brown, Yellow and in-between in America, it is our land too and we are here to stay.

It was no accident that we are here in America; God does not deal in accidents. We are here by a Divine Plan and only God knows the answer to the Final Plan for His Black people. We must try to learn to work and live together.

PART II

Black Men in a White World

News, books and other Medias are saying that African Americans are too sensitive about racial attitude in White America. That Black people should get over it. Many do not believe that black people, especially black males are targeted because they are black. Some naive people believe that in these United States all are equal. Some ignorant blacks and whites buy into this myth. The after math of slavery still exists in this country. The Church has worked to some extent to help in this situation but the residuals of racism still exist.

We can see the effects of racism by the number of black men and youth who are in the Penal System and who are shot just because they are black. White Police Officers have no respect for Black people. Many believe that the only good black man is one looking from behind prison, jail bars or six feet under. As we look at statistics, white males do the same things as blacks but are less likely to end up in the penal system as are black males. If white males are arrested, their time in jail is much less than blacks who commit the same crimes. I repeat the saying; black men and now women are arrested while driving black or shot just because they are black.

Police are taught to target blacks because they consider them high crime risk makers. White thieves are ravaging the country and corporate America but nothing is done to them. As Christians we are obliged to teach our youth how to live in a racist system to avoid some of those actions which would land them in jail whether they are guilty or not. We also have to teach our male youths to love themselves and to love one another.

We alone cannot change the system. This is our country too. Our ancestors help build this country with the sweat of their brow. Pastors can help the situation by providing aggressive Youth Programs to educate our young men to deal with the situation from the perspective of Jesus. Jesus was a peace-maker and taught us to love everyone. However, if our youths see other divisive actions by the Church then no amount of catechesis will make them better because they will think that the Church is not sincere.

Not everyone on the Police force is racists but there are enough in the Police Department to make the life of black men miserable and feel less like men. Not knowing when a Policeman will draw a gun and start shooting without probable cause is scary, not only to black men but black women and children. God expects each of us to love one another as He loves us. Jesus came from heaven to set us all free from sin and death. Living life in such turmoil is not very reassuring.

The Church and the Black Community

The Church teaches that we should follow these same principles of Jesus. One of the things we can do is to get involved whenever there is an opportunity to attend meetings to address these hate issues and get involved in the process. As the Cardinals prepared to elect a new Pope, one wonders how many even considered an African for pope. Sometimes one wonders if their mentality of Jim Crow in America is prevalent over the whole world even entrenching itself into the Church founded by Jesus Christ. There were three Black Popes early in the life of the Church. How many African American would be considering to be elected as Cardinal? What is it with these white men and their reluctance to be fair and above board? To be fair there are many good and holy white churchman but because of the culture of denigrating black people, many do not give it much thought.

Many Catholics are wondering when we will be getting more Black Bishops. Many of our Black bishops are either dead or aged. At this writing there are only two black Bishops in charge of Dioceses. The others are auxiliary Bishops. Their jobs are compared to that of a Monsignor which is an honorary position. In some dioceses Deacons seems to have more clout. We talk about white policemen and their treatment of our black men; we have to also take a good look at the Catholic Church.

It is time for Black Catholics to make their voices heard in Rome about the lack of Blacks Bishops in the United States. Why are we so hesitant to make our needs known? What can the Church do to us? This is the Church of Jesus Christ. "We as a people have been to the Mountain Top" to quote Martin Luther King, Jr. Let us not be afraid.

"Saying you are sorry, for a bad deed, does not make it so... the devil was sorry too, but was denied heaven…let us be honest and change."

Grow Not Weary

(Senryu)

When we grow weary
Of our journey in this life
Look to our Anchor.

God will be our strength,
Our rampart and our bulwark
Trust only in Him.

We can count on God
To be there in times of great trials
Trust Him at all times.

So grow not weary
Of tribulations and stress,
God is our stronghold.

Immigrants

Even natural born citizens have ancestors who migrated from other countries; with one exception. The only exception was the introduction of slavery into the mainstream of the Colonies. Thus, no one who lives in these United States of America can really call anyone immigrants because all of their ancestors were immigrants. No one, according to historians, were here first except the Indians; but… according to historians, the Indians came from across the Bering Straits. Thus, if this is true, we all are truly immigrants. This country was uninhabited. The Indians came first, then the Europeans, then by force the Africans. The Asian and other nationalities arrived later. So what gives us the right to determine who can reside here or not? Since we do live in a democracy, laws have to be made to protect the country and its citizens. Because some people have forgotten from whence we all originated, laws were made by a choice few about who should and should not live in these United States of America.

We forget that God is the creator of this world. God created us and all that is in it. As Christians, we believe that all peoples are created equal by God and that we are all children of that same God. If this is so, then we cannot discriminate against immigrants who are coming to this country wanting a better life for themselves and their families. Our government, however, has to be cautious about allowing people into the country who wish to overthrow the government or perform some type of terrorism or mayhem.

As African Americans whose ancestors were brought to these United States by force as slaves from Africa, it would be totally unchristian to even think of discriminating against immigrants. Had the United

States refused to allow Servant of God, Mother Mary Lange and others who joined her into this country, there would be no Oblate Sisters of Providence. A significant number of scientists and engineers were foreign born who have made a significant impact in making the United States a Super Power. Slave labor and Immigrants from all walks of life made this country truly great, coming from all educational and religious backgrounds.

God expects us to be as gracious to the immigrants as he has been to us. As African Americans we can relate to being hated for being different from the dominant race. African Americans embraced the Catholic Church knowing that it had flaws. The Catholic Church was not about the dominant race but about God who has control over all creation and that he will reward all of us for our faithfulness to Him. Jesus came on earth to redeem all humankind and he expects us to love each other in spite of our differences. We need to get over our dread of different races and other cultures. It is because we are all different that we can complement each other through our racial chrisms. All nationalities are children of God. We must all be welcome guests at the table.

HONORING OUR CATECHISTS

CHAPTER 13

Kingdom Building is never Done

A Reflection

Living the Proclaimed Word

Catechists are dedicated to Service

Each year the Church honors all Catechetical Ministers by dedicating a special Sunday in their honor, recalling the selfless dedication of men and women all across the nation and the Christian world. Catechists take seriously the admonition of Christ to heart, as he commissioned the Apostles, "Go therefore, and make disciples of all nations." (Matt.28 19) This mandate of Christ to "teach all nations" overrides any nationalism or territorial boundaries. We define catechesis as echoing and reechoing the words of God in our communities, telling about God the Father, God the Son and the blessed Holy Spirit as they influence the connection of families and communities, entrenching them in their faith. Therefore, it is fitting that we have a special time each year, when these unselfish women and men can be recognized and shown appreciation for all that they do.

It is of paramount importance that catechesis and the Word be taught simultaneously. Why? Because they complement one another in the strictest form or sense… the Word is that which saves and gives life to the Christian. It supplies the yeast that binds peoples together as followers of Christ. It is the Word which gives impetus to the meaning of being a true Christian. Catechists are those people who impart the concept *catechesis* and enlarge on the Word which saves. Catechists are carriers of the Word.

Proclamation of the Word is serious business putting the catechists on the spot, since they are the keepers, proclaimers and doers of the Word. Since catechists know the seriousness of these two principles, they continue to catechize. Although the task is serious, yet they strive to do their very best. Children, youth and adults receive the best Christian education that they as ministers of Christ, can afford.

The Church relies on catechists to impart the faith to the faithful in spite of the other tasks that the catechist has to do on a daily basis: take care of family, aged parents and the like. They are not looking for an earthly reward but one that will last forever. Catechists are real apostles. They are Disciples of Christ who have dedicated their lives to service as did the Apostles and disciples long, long ago. St. Paul says it well in his letter to Timothy, "If we have died with Christ, we shall also live with him, if we persevere, we shall also reign with him" (2 Timothy 2: 11-12).

Catechists know that imparting the faith to the Church of Christ takes time and energy. In order to do a good job they have to be fortified by being prayerful and steeped in the Spirit. It is a total dying to self, becoming other Christ. There is a saying that, "You cannot give what you haven't got." If catechists expect to lead others to Christ, their lives must be up to par. They must feed daily on the Word by prayer and daily meditation. Christ expects catechist to be holy people so that those they catechize might see Jesus in them. Relying on God's infinite grace and divine mercy, we can do all things and do them well because God has our back.

St. Paul, again in his second letter to Timothy, gives us something to think about when he says, "All Scripture is inspired by God and is useful for teaching, for refutation, for correction, for training in righteousness, so that one who belongs to God may be competent, and equipped for every good work " (2 Timothy 4: 16-17). Following this, we can always work with blessed assurance that working for God will in the end reap its own reward, eternal life.

Catechists are usually people who have full time jobs, although there are many who are retired and desire to give something back… and so they serve. The most amazing aspect of these wonderful people is that they recognize and appreciate the power of God in their lives, thus they serve as teachers; testifying to God's goodness, mercy and compassion. They teach, because they cannot help themselves and impelled to serve.

In their service, they sacrifice time from family as they prepare lessons, meet students, parents and undergo training and enrichment classes. Yet, in some parishes or schools not much thought or thanks are given to catechists. Often they are the invisible people, but God sees and that is all that matters. Most catechists minister for 10, 20, and 30 years or more, all for the love of Jesus.

Catechists are teachers, doctors, lawyers, psychologists, store managers, principal, clerks, mothers, fathers; just to name a few of the people who are volunteers. These selfless volunteers give up their time and energy, week after week to work for the Church. They have everyday J.O.B.S. After work they come to where the real JOB is the JESUS ministry. It is these ministers who bring the Good News of Jesus, Sunday after Sunday as well as weekdays in evening classes and the RCIA to the People of God.

Many use their own resources to fulfill their mission and often, in some of our parishes, classrooms are make-shift. They know how to "make do." These are the spirit-filled people who are so creative and dedicated. Catechetical Sunday is an opportunity to draw attention to the ministry of catechesis and to the extraordinary people who serve in this ministry. Let us encourage them to "Keep On Teaching" so that the Word of God may spread far and wide.

Where would the Church be without these dedicated ministers? They are indeed true disciples who heeded the call of the Jesus, "To go out into the world and spread the Good News" (Mark 28:19-20). This dedication to spread the Good News is demanding and sometimes stressful as these women and men struggle to keep families and ministries running smoothly. Somehow, God sees their sacrifices and gives them, as well as family members, the ability and the skills to cope with their situation.

Catechists are people who proclaim the Word of God, of Jesus, and the Holy Spirit. Catechists also teach the tenants of the faith and connect it to the larger community of the faithful. Catechists know that what God promised to our ancestors is also promised to us. They in turn pass this knowledge on to those they teach. In each ethnic Community, the Catechist connects the heritage of those they catechize to the teachings of the Church. Catechists also teach that the Church is all about relationship; it is about our relationship with God the Father, the Son, the Holy Spirit and with each other. This relationship is to be continued throughout the week, in the workplace, in school and all social interactions.

A CATECHIST is …

A – Available to God

C - Conscientious to ministry
A - Ability to handle any situation
T - Teacher of Catechesis
E - Enabler of the People of God
C - Christian who motivates
H - Happy doing the Work of the Lord
I - Intuitive in Ministry
S - Solicitous for others
T - Tolerable towards all

CHAPTER 14

Encountering Christ Changes the Catechist

"Encountering the Living Christ."

Encountering the living Christ is no ordinary encounter, like the disciples on their way to Emmaus, it is one of profound joy and exhilaration. This Jesus, this Son of God, Son of Mary, took on mortal flesh to give us the opportunity to be like Him. Meeting Jesus, in our everyday lives, means to empty ourselves of all that is not of Him. We must know that we serve a living, triune God.

Catechists constantly encounter Christ by doing the ministry that is so dear to the heart of them all. Children and adult alike would not know Jesus in an intimate and profound way was it not for these dedicated men and women who sacrifice time, talent, money and sometime health to do the work of the Lord.

Each encounter with one another should be a new and unique experience. For to meet each other on the spiritual level, increases our awareness of our connectedness to the other and to Christ. To operate separately from this mode is not in the Christian tradition. It breaks the unity. The human and divine encounter when it is broken, becomes something else entirely, self-centeredness. Here in the Archdiocese of Baltimore, Catechists, Youth, RCIA ministers are strongly urged to get certified. Our leaders want ministers of catechesis to be well prepared and fortified to strengthen the faith of the faithful both youth and adults. Catechetical ministers must be well equipped to defend and live their faith in a world which tell them through the media, radio, movies, newspapers and magazines that this world is all there is… period.

The faithful are urged to live life to the fullest, for there is only today. They would tell you that religion is not important. The youth are furthered bombarded by their unbelieving peers… if it feels good… then it is good. Those women and men who are responsible for the faith formation of the Church have a tremendous responsibility to be true evangelizers and that is no easy task.

Women and men share their knowledge and love of God through their total abandonment with a deep reliance on our provident God to walk with then in their ministry. They encounter Christ in the constant preparation for the work of ministry. Often they are given the opportunity to participate in retreats to refresh and renew their souls for they know they cannot give what they do not possess. Workshops give them the opportunity to learn how to best impart the faith experience to those they serve.

Encountering Christ is one of service, once you meet Jesus and get to know him you are impelled to run and tell somebody. No one can remain the same after they have met Jesus. Thus ministry takes on a supernatural tone

Encountering Christ gives them a new walk, a new talk, and a totally different attitude. Catechists take on a new glow, people look at them in a different way. Many say, "Hey I want what they've got, I want to be like them," and so others join the rank of Catechetical ministers. Encountering Christ is like a stone tossed into the water, the water ripples out as far as the eye can see and beyond, that is what encountering Christ mean. So they are prodded to continue to be ripples in their ministry as they encounter the living Christ each day of the year.

Encountering Christ

Women and men of all ages and states
Leave home... bring Jesus... tells of his glory.
Week days and Sundays' lessons are first rate
Seeks creative ways... telling the story

A Bible in hand and a small brief case
They head out to conquer for Christ, their rock.
It matter not the place or grim the face
They bring the gospel to God's little flock.

Encountering Christ has given the strength
To rely on providence too, for their grace
To seek always the greater good at length
And to be anchored as they run the race.

We all encounter Christ through each other
When we meet our sisters and our brothers
Day after day and Sunday after Sunday
In a genuine Christian way.

Who Do You Say That I Am?

"Who do you say that I am" is still a valid question for us today. Jesus asked that question of his disciples over two thousand years ago. We too can respond as did Peter, "You are the Christ, the Son of the living God" (Matt.16: 16). By our very baptism we are all called to answer that question. How do "*we*" react to this question of Jesus? As Christian women and men who are called to bring others to Jesus. How do we do this? We do this by paying attention to the People of God; wherever we are at every moment of every day of our lives.

We are all called to discipleship and as disciples are called to evangelize, to bring others to the Jesus and the Kingdom. Catechists, true disciples, bring the Word of God to children and adults. The primary ministry of Catechists is to evangelize. Although the Church says that the Bishops are the primary ministers who see that the process of the faith is carried forth, yet it is left to the grass roots, Catechists, to actually take the Word out among God's people. They do this in schools, Catechetical Centers, homes, Parish Centers, College Campuses and the like. They echo and re-echo the word of God, to the community of believers and others who do not yet believe.

Catechists are true disciples who, like the disciples of old, worked without ceasing, with no remuneration and sometimes with little thanks. They are volunteers who know that their reward will come from God. They are co-workers with God. How awesome it is to be a co-worker with the Creator!

The Church in this modern technological world calls each of us to be evangelizers. It seems that our Catechists have been doing this long, long before the word "evangelization" became so popular in our society. To evangelize means to bring the message of God to those who do not know God, those who have forgotten God and those who are indifferent to God and to continue to urge those who are converted to keep on keeping on.

Evangelization and catechesis go hand in hand. How we have separated them for so long is a great mystery. Actually, they have not been separated; we just did not name or claim the connection until now. The connection was always there.

As we continue to ponder the words of Jesus, "Who do you say that I am" Catechists acknowledge that Jesus is Lord and worthy to be praised in song, words and deeds. The question really is one of action. We are to act on these words of Jesus and Catechists have taken these words to heart and acted upon them.

How do Catechists act on these words of Jesus? They show up Sunday, after Sunday, after Sunday as well as weekdays and weekends.

What drives these women and men to do what they do year in and year out? It is called love of Jesus and dedication to their Church. They are about "KINGDOM BUILDING." It is about a commitment of service to children and adults. It is not about who is in charge. We all know who is ultimately in charge. God! We are only instruments to be used for the glory of God and the good of God's people.

Who do you say that I am? Jesus you are the Christ, the Son of the living and eternal God, our Savior, our brother and our friend. We praise you; we worship you through ministry to your children no matter what age or stage of development. We ask You, Lord, to continue to use us.

USE US LORD

Use us Lord:

Like Mary of Nazareth, Mother of Jesus.
Like you used the Apostles Peter and Paul.

Use us Lord:

Like you used James, John and Silas
Like you used Mother Mary Lange and Father Joubert.

Use us Lord:

Like those men and women on whose shoulders we now stand.
Like you used the Saints past and present.

Use us Lord:

Like a favorite passage in the Bible.
Like a good sermon on Sunday morning.

Use us Lord.

Like musical instruments…
Use us! Yes, Lord,
Use us.

MARY… MOTHER OF JESUS AND OUR MOTHER

CHAPTER 15

The Black Madonnas

Allegany Arts

During the month of May, we celebrate Mary, the Mother of Jesus. During this season, churches provide services of special devotion to Our Lady. Often, a litany of names honoring the Madonna is recited in prayer asking Our Lady to pray for us.

There, is also a litany of names of black Madonnas, less mentioned yet worthy of our reverence as we pray.

History records that the first known "black Madonna" came out of Egypt named Isis. Isis was a goddess, wife and sister of Osiris. She was known as the goddess of fertility, often depicted holding her son Horus to her breast. Isis was the prototype of the Virgin Mary, the Mother of Jesus.

The pre-Christian ancient Roman army had a great devotion to Isis, carrying her statue into battle as a means of protection and prayed to her for victory over their enemies. When the Romans left Europe, shrines to Isis were left behind, thus perpetuating her image. Although of pre-Christian origin, Isis is considered the first black Madonna. From this concept other black Madonnas surfaced

During the Crusades, the Templars brought back images of black Madonnas with them from the areas of Ethiopia and Egypt. Many believed that these black Madonnas have great healing power and are able to work great miracles. Although the majority of the Madonnas are called black, there are other Madonnas of color such as "Our Lady of Guadalupe."

In South America there are black as well as brown Madonnas. The majority of black Madonnas have Negroid features. There seems to be a resurgence of devotion to black Madonnas all over the world. From the beginning the Madonnas usually looked liked the people of the land where they originated, namely Ethiopia and Egypt.

However, during the Middle Ages, the West adapted the idea of Mary and Jesus as Madonna and Child from Isis and Horus when Europe was Christianized. Perhaps many of the early sculptures and artists got the idea to do their work in black from Scripture in the book of "Song of Songs", which says, "I am black, but beautiful (Song of Songs 1:5). The fact that these Madonna were black did not hinder reverence given to them in the past. Some of these black Madonnas are still visible while others are stored in caves or lower chapels.

Although some church leaders were ordered to "whiten" a great majority of the black Madonnas, my research indicates an irony that people around the world still favored these black Madonnas giving them reverence and honor.

France has over 300 black Virgin sites naming 150 of these as black Madonnas. Other European countries such as Spain, Italy, Germany, Belgium, Portugal, Russia, and Switzerland have black Madonnas.

Many Black Madonnas from these countries are named after the locale where a chapel is erected, such as Our Lady of Loretto, Italy. In Brazil, one such Madonna is "Our Lady of Aparedida." In Cuba and Central America, "Our Lady of Charity is depicted as a black Madonna.

There are white Madonnas blackened by age, candle smoke and fire. Some were buried during times of war and persecution, thus becoming black. It is said that when these Madonnas were restored to their whiteness many people preferred the black Madonna. Many claimed that their prayers were answered faster in the black depiction.

Black Madonnas were here long, long before the present Madonnas often seen gracing our churches. This is truth and this is history.

The devotion to Mary Mother of Jesus is a popular act of piety in the African-American Catholic Community. Hopefully we can now add to our Litany some of the Black Madonnas of Our Lady of Peace and Good Voyage (Antipollo City, Philippines), Our Lady of Charity (Cuba and Central Americans), Our Lady of Loretto (Italy) and Our Lady, Mother of Africa (statue found in a lower chapel of the National Shrine of the Immaculate Mary in Washington, DC, promoted and established by African American Catholics of the United States).

Mary, Mother of Jesus and Our Mother

The month of May is dedicated to Mary, the Mother of Jesus and our Mother. Mary, outside of the Trinity, is the closest to her Son, Jesus. We know that a mother has a tender heart and since Jesus gave Mary to us while hanging on that awful cross on Good Friday, she had accepted all of us as her children.

Therefore, as her children she will care for us in the same manner and degree that she cared for Jesus. She will be attentive to our needs and even our wants. Remember you own parents or guardian how much they loved you and tried to fulfill all of your requests. That is the kind of parent Mary is.

Mary will not give us things that will harm us but if it is something for our own good and holiness be assured that you will get your request. Good mothers are full of compassion and love so we look to this good mother for favors from her Son Jesus.

Holy Mary Mother of God, pray for us sinners, as we face the trials and tribulations of a fallen world each day. Remain with us at the hour of our death as you were with Joseph and Jesus at the hour of their deaths. Amen.

MARY

MOTHER OF JESUS

Mary, Mother of Jesus and our mother
Hear us when we pray to you…

Sometimes
We ask for worldly things or things that
Are not good for our spiritual well being.
Being the good mother that you are
You know our needs far better than we.

Please be patient with us
When we ask for childish things
Give us what we need,
As we need it, when we need it.

Relying on the graces
Of your most generous Son Jesus,
We ask for many blessings.
Amen.

A Reflection on the Magnificat of Mary

Mary's proclamation of praise is one we can attest to as people of color. For the Lord has indeed done great things for us and holy is God's name. God lifted us up from slavery, Jim Crow, to the Civil Rights Movement to our present day battle against subtle racism in our workplace, our Church and our Country. We have been given the strength to continue the battle. We know from whence we came and must strive to maintain our trust in God, as Mary trusted.

We can claim the promise that God made to our ancestors and to our father in faith Abraham and our mother Sarah and all our ancestors. For what our God promised to the Israelites, he also promised to us. All we have to do is to claim our heritage and have faith in the promise. God does not promise what God can not deliver.

When times get tough and the going gets rough and we do not know where to turn; look to Mary, the mother of Jesus, for the strength to go on. Remember what Mary said, "God's faithful love extends from age to age." Can we relate to these sentiments of Mary? How?

Hail Mary

Hail to you Mary, mother of God
All the earth tells of your worth
Into the world came Jesus the Jesse rod
Leaving heaven to come to earth.

Mothering Jesus was your main thrust
Allowing us to gain a seat in heaven
Releasing us from sin and gain firm trust
Yes was your answer for us as our leaven.

OUR LADY OF MOUNT PROVIDENCE

A MEDITATION

(AN ACROSTIC)

O – OPEN

Mary was open to the Holy Spirit, saying yes when asked to be the Mother of Jesus.
Are we like Mary, open to the Holy Spirit in our daily lives? If not why not?

U - USABLE

Mary could be used by God anytime simply by her yes to God. Leaving her childhood was not easy. What about me, can God use me anytime without any reservations?

R - RELIABLE

Mary was reliable, her yes meant yes then and forever. What about my yes? Can God count on me to be reliable?

L - LOVING

Mary loving and lovable at all times, in good times and bad. How can I imitate Mary in her way of loving?

A - AVAILABLE

All during her life, Mary was available to God. What about my availability to God, to my Parish Community, my workplace, to all the people of God, if a religious, my congregation?

D - DUTIFUL

Mary was dutiful in saying yes to God and being a good wife to Joseph. As a wife she had many duties and tasks to accomplish, yet she carried all of these through with love. What can I do to imitate Mary in being dutiful as a member of the Household of God?

Y - YIELDING

It was not easy being a teenager, wife and mother, yet Mary managed. What ways can I be yielding to God in my daily living, in the workplace, in my ministry?

O - OPTAMISTIC

Mary was very optimistic. She could not see the whole picture of God's plan for her, however, she trusted in God's Providence. Just how optimistic am I in my reliance on Divine Providence?

F - FEARLESS

Mary was fearless because she knew that God was at her back. Do you feel that you can do anything, be anything because God has your back?

P - PROTECTOR

Mary was the protector and provider for Jesus. Young, but strong in her resolve and in her love of God and willing to do God's will, she took on the awesome task. What about me, how strong and resolve am I in my love of Jesus?

R - RESOURCEFUL

Mary was not rich, she married a poor carpenter, yet she managed a loving home for her family. What about me, what kind of loving atmosphere do I provide in my job, my ministry or religious family? Am I self-giving?

O - ORDERLY

Mary was not only open to the Spirit; she also had an orderly mind. Although a housewife, she found time to pray as well as work. How do I plan my time? Do I take time to focus on both prayer and work, giving prayer my priority?

V - VIRTUOUS

Mary led a virtuous life. She knew from childhood that she belonged to God and lived her life according to that principle. I am also called to live a virtuous life. How do I measure up in this regards? Is there something in my life that has to change?

I - INVIOLATE

Mary, a virgin lived with Joseph without compromising her virginity. God calls all Christians to live a chaste and inviolate life. Some Christians are chaste from the beginning; others become so because they love the Lord. It is said that, "The eye is the window of the Soul." How do I measure up to being inviolate? What does our reading, Television, videos and DVD's consist? Would we be ashamed to ask Jesus to be our companion during these times?

D - DESTINED

Destined from all ages to be the Mother of God, Mary stated her humility in her Magnificent. She did not boast but expressed her lowliness. For what am I destined? How can I determine my destiny? Or can I?

E - ENDURING

Mary's enduring love for God was her continued faithfulness to her yes to be the Mother of the Messiah. How enduring is my love for my God? Have I taken anything back after saying yes to the Lord at my First Communion, Confirmation, wedding or vow day? Think about it!

N - NOBILITY

Nobility was one of the virtues of Mary. She gained the title when she became the Mother of Jesus, the King of Heaven and Earth. I belong to the nobility as well, for I am a child of King Jesus. Have I acted like a kid of the King? Will people see in my actions or demeanor that I come from nobility?

C - CHASTE

Mary was chaste even before she was born. She was freed from all sin since she was to be the Mother of God. I was born with original sin, but baptized into grace and became clean. How can I live a chaste life in an unchaste world?

E—ENDURANCE

Mary had an enduring love of God. She endured all the heartaches God sent her. The humiliation of having Jesus, the Son of God, born in a stable, fleeing her homeland to Egypt., losing Jesus for three days in Jerusalem. Seeing her beloved Son, Jesus beaten, kicked, mocked while carrying his splinter filled cross to Calvary and watching Jesus nailed to the cross. Mary's heart was pierced through, seeing Jesus die a slow agonizing death and not being able to help ease the pain. Mary knew that all of this suffering was a part of God's plan for her. What about me, what is my endurance level? Do I forgive like Jesus and Mary? Or when things go wrong for me do I retaliate?

PRAYER: Lord, help me to be like you and your Mother Mary. Give me the strength to be courageous in all the circumstances of life. Let me forgive when I am humiliated, to be kind when I am slighted, to be generous when I am ignored. Lord, let me be like you and your Mother Mary. Life was not easy for either of you, so when my life gets rough let me remember how much you loved us Jesus to give your life for us and to imitate you Mary who said yes when you did not know the outcome of your situation. Let me trust the Father and blessed Holy Spirit to be there for me too, in all my situations. Amen.

I Prayed the Rosary Today

I prayed the Rosary today,
For all the ills in this world
That peace will reign all over
In Iraq, Syria and Afghanistan.

I prayed the rosary today
For aborted babies from rejected wombs
That was made for love but now at war
With murder replacing mother love.

I prayed the rosary today,
For families to raise good children
That love and respect each other
And love the neighbor as themselves.

I prayed the rosary today,
For all those in need
Of any prayers at all
That God would keep then in His care.

I prayed the rosary today,
For leaders to make wise decisions
Decisions that bring peace and harmony
To all the peoples in every land.

I prayed the rosary today,
That people all over the universe
Would turn to God and pray
Through all the situations in their lives,
I prayed the rosary today.

SAINT JOSEPH THE WORKER

Guardian of Jesus and Mary

Allegany Arts

St. Joseph is called the worker and so we might give him this title. However, Joseph was more than a worker. He was the protector of the Child Jesus and his wife Mary, the mother of Jesus. God the Father gave Joseph a grave responsibility. He was a provider not only of food, clothing, shelter and protection but provided the family with love, peace and joy. St Joseph provided sustainability and cohesiveness to that little family. We can be sure he did "WORK" at being the best husband and father he could be. Saint Joseph can be a model for all men and boys. By following his example, we all can become better persons. Trust Saint Joseph as he was trusted by God, to care for his Son, Jesus. Not much is known about this man Joseph, whom God chose to be the guardian of His Son Jesus and Mary the Mother of this Son. What we do know is that he was a just man. When Mary was found with child through the power of the Holy Spirit it was the custom to stone such a woman. She had no husband and here she was pregnant.

Through reflective prayer and trust in God; God revealed to Joseph that this Child was His Son. Joseph obediently took Mary as his wife and cared for Jesus as if He was his natural son. As we read scripture we see that Joseph was a good father. We do not know just when he died. Jesus must have been a teenager because when the family went to Jerusalem to worship, as was the custom, when a young boy was twelve, he was presented again to the Lord.

Saint Joseph

Saint Joseph husband of Mary
And foster father of Jesus, the boy.
Be a father to us as we mature,
Help us be good and always pure.

Teach us to trust God always
As we set our hearts heaven-ward.
When it is time to close our eyes
To meet our Jesus, in the pale blue sky.

Take our hand and guide us
To our home above the clouds,
To sing God's glory forever
And ever in the celestial sky.

ABOUT THE BOOK

This book is about our union with God from a biblical and every day perspective as we interact with God and each other. Basically it speaks of basic truths as we live our lives out as Christians who believes that all races are intertwined since we all have the same Creator and that we should respect each other as children of the same Father. May we, as children of God, be willing to help one another to become better human beings. The book tries to show that we must love and respect one another because we are all precious in the eyes of God.

ABOUT THE AUTHOR

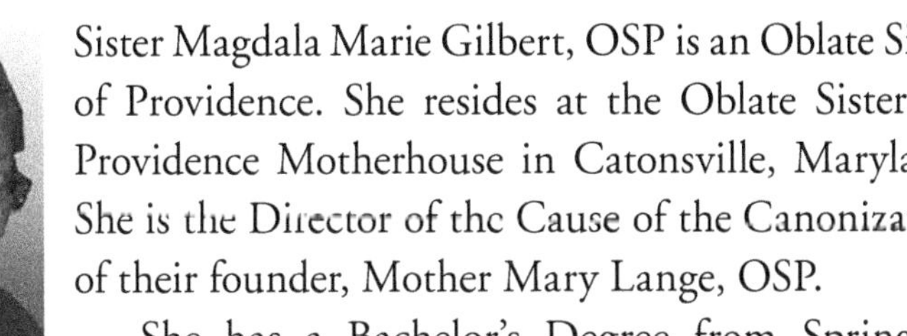

Sister Magdala Marie Gilbert, OSP is an Oblate Sister of Providence. She resides at the Oblate Sisters of Providence Motherhouse in Catonsville, Maryland. She is the Director of the Cause of the Canonization of their founder, Mother Mary Lange, OSP.

She has a Bachelor's Degree from Springhill College in Mobile, Alabama, a Master's Degree from Towson University, Towson, Maryland. She is a Notary Public. Sister has a Professional Catechetical Certificate from the Archdiocese of Baltimore and a Professional Catechist Certificate from the Imani Program from the Institute of Black Catholic Studies, Xavier University in New Orleans, Louisiana.

CPSIA information can be obtained
at www.ICGtesting.com
Printed in the USA
BVHW071136040319
541705BV00009B/176/P

9 781796 015355